Crafted by 40! Art of My Life

SANDESH SIDDARAM

Made with ❤ on the Notion Press Platform

www.notionpress.com

For My Children, so they will know

Special thanks to my parents, wife, teachers, mentors, reporting managers, friends, colleagues and my beloved community

Contents

Just Right Click and Refresh !!!

As I sit here, in a quiet corner of my favourite spot, I find myself taking a deep breath and reflecting on the journey that has brought me to this moment. My name is Sandesh Siddaram, and on the 10th of September 2024, I will turn 40 years old. This upcoming milestone feels like a natural time to pause and look back on the road I've travelled, the experiences I've lived through, and the lessons I've learned along the way.

This book is essentially a conversation with myself. It's a dialogue between the Sandesh of today and the Sandesh of the past. Over the years, I've gathered a collection of 40 key learnings, and each one of these has its own chapter in this book. Each chapter tells a story, shares an experience, and highlights a moment that changed the way I see the world. These aren't just lessons—they are the very essence of my journey, the core values that have shaped who I am today.

I like to think of myself as a "Valuepreneur," a term I use to describe someone who adds value not just to their own life but also to the lives of others. Through this book, I aim to share that value with you. This isn't just a gift to myself as I approach my 40th birthday; it's also a gift to you, the reader. My hope is that through the stories and reflections in these pages, you might find some inspiration, some motivation, and perhaps even a few lessons that you can apply to your own life.

Purpose of Writing This Book

Turning 40 feels like a significant turning point in my life. It's a time to pause, reflect, and take stock of everything that has brought me to this moment. For me, this book is a way to do just that. It's a deeply personal project, one that I've poured my heart into. It's a celebration of the life I've lived so far—the highs and the lows, the successes and the setbacks, and most importantly, the wisdom I've gained along the way.

The purpose of this book can be summed up in three main ideas:

1. Self-Reflection:

Writing this book has given me the chance to look back on my life with a sense of gratitude and understanding. It's allowed me to acknowledge the experiences that have shaped me, the challenges I've faced, and the lessons I've learned. This process of reflection has been like having a conversation with myself—a chance to sit down, take a deep breath, and truly appreciate the journey that has brought me here.

2. Inspiration for Others:

While this book is deeply personal, it's also meant to be a source of inspiration and motivation for others. Life is a series of lessons, and each one of those lessons has the power to change us for the better. By sharing my stories and insights, I hope to offer something valuable to you, the reader. Maybe you'll find a story that resonates with you, or a lesson that speaks to something you're going through in your own life. My goal is to add value to your journey, just as my experiences have added value to mine.

3. Legacy:

Finally, this book is about leaving something meaningful behind. It's a record of my thoughts, my values, and my experiences. It's my way of contributing to the world, of adding value in a way that goes beyond my own life. I hope that this book will continue to inspire and motivate others long after I'm gone. In that sense, it's a legacy, something that I can leave behind as a testament to the life I've lived and the lessons I've learned.

As you read through these pages, I invite you to join me on this journey of reflection and discovery. Imagine us sitting together in a peaceful place, sharing stories, and thinking about life. My hope is that my experiences will resonate with you, that my lessons will inspire you, and that my journey will somehow add value to yours. I'm grateful that you're here, that you're taking the time to read my story, and that you're allowing me to share it with you.

Curtain Raiser

Life is full of ups and downs, and my journey has been no different. Over the years, I've faced challenges that tested my resolve, celebrated successes that filled me with pride, and experienced moments of quiet reflection that helped me grow as a person. As I approach 40, I realize that each of these experiences has played a crucial role in shaping who I am today. One of the most important lessons I've learned is the value of self-reflection. Taking the time to look back on our lives, to understand where we've been and how we've grown, is essential for personal development. It's easy to get caught up in the hustle and bustle of everyday life, but I've found that pausing to reflect on my experiences has allowed me to gain a deeper understanding of myself and the world around me.

Self-reflection has also helped me appreciate the importance of gratitude. When I look back on my life, I'm filled with a sense of thankfulness for the people who have supported me, the opportunities I've been given, and the lessons I've learned along the way. Gratitude has become a guiding principle in my life, one that I strive to practice every day.

Another key lesson I've learned is the power of resilience. Life is unpredictable, and we all face challenges that test our strength and determination. Over the years, I've encountered my fair share of obstacles, but each time I've been knocked down, I've found the strength to get back up. This resilience has been a driving force in my life, pushing me to keep moving forward even when the going gets tough.

Resilience is closely tied to another important value: perseverance. There have been times when I've felt like giving up, when the challenges I faced seemed insurmountable. But I've learned that perseverance—keeping going even when things are difficult—is key to achieving our goals. It's not always easy, but the rewards are worth the effort.

Throughout my life, I've also come to understand the significance of authenticity. Being true to ourselves, living in alignment with our values, and not being afraid to show the world who we really are—these are essential for living a fulfilling life. Authenticity has been a guiding principle for me, and it's something I strive to embody in everything I do.

Of course, no journey is complete without the people we meet along the way. I've been fortunate to have been surrounded by supportive friends, family, and mentors who have played a significant role in my life. These relationships have taught me the importance of connection, of building strong, meaningful bonds with the people around us. It's through these connections that we find support, love, and a sense of belonging.

As I reflect on my journey, I'm also reminded of the importance of continuous learning. Life is a never-ending process of growth and development, and there's always something new to learn. I've found that staying curious, being open to new experiences, and seeking out opportunities for growth have been key to my personal and professional success.

This book is a celebration of all these lessons and more. It's a tribute to the life I've lived, the challenges I've faced, and the wisdom I've gained along the way. But more than that, it's a gift to you, the reader. I hope that by sharing my stories, I can offer something valuable to you, something that will inspire you on your own journey.

As I look ahead to the future, I'm filled with a sense of excitement and anticipation. I know that there are still many lessons to be learned, challenges to be faced, and experiences to be had. But I also know that with each new chapter, I'll continue to grow, evolve, and add value to my life and the lives of others.

Thank you for joining me on this journey. I'm honored to share my story with you, and I hope that it will resonate with you in some way. Whether you're at a crossroads in your own life, looking for inspiration, or simply reflecting on your own journey, I hope that these pages will offer you something of value.

As we continue this journey together, I invite you to reflect on your own life, to consider the lessons you've learned, and to think about the value you can add to your own life and the lives of others. After all, life is a journey, and we're all in this together.

Sandesh Siddaram

10th September 2024

Value 1 - Which YUGA are we in? AGE of Self Reflection

In Sanatana Dharma, time is divided into four great ages or "Yugas." Each Yuga represents a different stage of the world's spiritual and moral evolution. The four Yugas are Krita Yuga, Treta Yuga, Dvapara Yuga, and Kali Yuga. Each has its own characteristics, stories, and lessons, reflecting the journey of the universe and the souls within it. The Yugas are like chapters in a cosmic book, each with its own challenges and opportunities for growth.

Today, we find ourselves in Kali Yuga, often referred to as the Age of Self-Reflection. This is an era unlike any other, where the greatest battles are not fought on battlefields or against external enemies, but within our own minds and hearts. Understanding this Yuga, and its significance, can offer us profound insights into the nature of our struggles, the importance of self-awareness, and the path to personal growth.

The Four Yugas: A Brief Overview

Before diving into Kali Yuga, let's briefly explore the other three Yugas to understand the progression of time and spiritual evolution in Sanatana Dharma thought.

1. Krita Yuga (Satya Yuga) – The Golden Age: Krita Yuga, also known as Satya Yuga, is the first and most perfect age. This is the age of truth and righteousness, where divine beings walk the earth, and there is no trace of evil or suffering. In this era, dharma (moral order) is fully established, and everyone lives in harmony with the laws of the universe. It's a time of purity, where human beings are at their highest potential, fully aware of their divine nature. There are no conflicts, and the world is in perfect balance.

2. Treta Yuga – The Age of Heroes: Treta Yuga is the age of great kings and epic battles, most famously represented by the story of Rama and Ravana. In this age, the fight between good and evil manifests on a grand scale, with human heroes like Lord Rama confronting powerful demons like Ravana. This Yuga is marked by the decline of dharma; only three-quarters of it remains. The challenges of this era involve external battles, where the forces of good must defeat the forces of evil to restore balance to the world.

3. Dvapara Yuga – The Age of Dharma: Dvapara Yuga is the age of duality, where the struggle between good and evil becomes more complex. It is the era of the Mahabharata, where the battle is not just between humans and demons but between members of the same family. The story of the Pandavas and the Kauravas illustrates the moral and ethical dilemmas that arise when family loyalties and personal ambitions conflict with dharma. In Dvapara Yuga, only half of dharma remains, and the world is marked by confusion, dishonesty, and a gradual decline in spiritual values.

4. Kali Yuga – The Age of Self-Reflection: Finally, we arrive at Kali Yuga, the age we are currently living in. This is the age of darkness and ignorance, where only one-quarter of dharma remains. The world in Kali Yuga is filled with moral decay, corruption, and suffering. However, unlike the previous Yugas, where the battles were fought against external enemies, the real battle in Kali Yuga is internal. It is a fight within us, a constant struggle between our higher and lower selves, between good and evil within our own minds.

The Unique Challenge of Kali Yuga: The Inner Battle

Kali Yuga is often viewed with a sense of foreboding, as it is described as an era of decline, where humanity drifts further away from dharma. However, it is also a time of great opportunity. In this age, the focus shifts from external conflicts to internal growth. The real challenge is not defeating demons or waging wars but mastering ourselves.

In Kali Yuga, the struggle is with our own minds and the negative tendencies that arise within us. These include greed, anger, jealousy, and ego. These internal enemies can be far more challenging to overcome than any external foe because they are deeply ingrained in our consciousness. The battle in this Yuga is ongoing, continuing until the end of our lives. It's a lifelong journey of self-reflection, self-discipline, and self-improvement.

The Power of Self-Reflection in Kali Yuga

In this age, self-reflection is not just important—it is essential. The battle within ourselves can only be won through deep introspection and an honest evaluation of our thoughts, actions, and desires. Self-reflection involves looking inwards, understanding our true nature, and striving to align our lives with higher values.

I've found that self-reflection is most effective when it is done regularly and intentionally. For me, this practice involves setting aside time each day to engage in a dialogue with myself. It's like holding a mirror up to my soul, examining what I see, and working to improve the areas where I fall short.

This practice is not about self-criticism or dwelling on mistakes; rather, it's about learning and growing. It's about asking ourselves important questions: What did I do today that aligns with my values? Where did I fall short? How can I improve tomorrow? This kind of self-reflection is a powerful tool for personal growth, helping us to stay on the right path, even in the midst of the challenges that Kali Yuga presents.

Engaging All Five Senses: The Practice of Self-Talk

One of the techniques I've developed over the years is speaking to myself out loud. This might sound unusual, but I've found it incredibly effective. By involving all five senses—seeing, hearing, touching, tasting, and smelling—we can deepen our self-reflection and make it more impactful.

For example, I often take a walk early in the morning, speaking out loud to myself as I go. This helps me to engage my sense of sight (as I observe the world around me), my sense of hearing (as I listen to my own voice), and my sense of touch (as I feel the ground beneath my feet). This multisensory approach makes the experience more real and helps me to process my thoughts more effectively.

Speaking out loud also has the benefit of making our thoughts more concrete. When we hear our own words, they take on a different meaning. It's one thing to think about our goals or challenges, but when we say them out loud, they become more tangible, more real. This practice also helps to clarify our thoughts, making it easier to identify where we need to focus our efforts.

The Daily Practice of Self-Reflection

In my own life, I've made self-reflection a daily practice. Every morning, I spend about 15 to 20 minutes speaking to myself, thinking about the day ahead, and reflecting on my goals and values. I also take a few minutes before bed to review the day, considering what went well, what didn't, and how I can improve.

This practice has been incredibly beneficial, helping me to stay grounded and focused, even in the midst of life's challenges. It has also helped me to develop a greater sense of self-awareness, which is essential in Kali Yuga. The more we understand ourselves—our strengths, weaknesses, desires, and fears—the better equipped we are to navigate the complexities of this age.

Preparing for Challenges: The Role of Self-Talk

Another important aspect of self-reflection in Kali Yuga is preparation. Life in this age is filled with challenges, and it's important to be prepared for them. One way I do this is by using self-talk as a form of rehearsal. Before any important presentation, meeting, or discussion, I take the time to speak to myself, going over what I want to say and how I want to say it.

This practice helps me to clarify my thoughts, organize my ideas, and build confidence. When the moment arrives, I feel more prepared, and my words tend to be more effective. This technique can be applied to any situation where we need to be at our best, whether it's a professional challenge, a personal conversation, or even just making an important decision.

The Continuous Battle: Mastering the Five Senses

One of the key lessons of Kali Yuga is the importance of mastering our five senses. In this age, our senses can easily lead us astray, pulling us towards desires, distractions, and behaviours that are not in line with our higher goals. The senses are powerful, and they can either be our greatest allies or our greatest enemies.

Mastering the senses doesn't mean denying them or suppressing them; rather, it means bringing them under control. It means developing the discipline to use our senses in a way that supports our personal growth, rather than undermining it. This is a continuous battle, one that requires constant vigilance and self-discipline.

For example, the sense of taste can lead us to overindulge in unhealthy foods, but it can also be harnessed to enjoy a balanced diet that nourishes the body and mind. The sense of sight can distract us with superficial pleasures, but it can also be used to appreciate the beauty and truth in the world around us. Each sense has the potential to either elevate or degrade us, depending on how we use it.

In my own life, I've found that mindfulness is key to mastering the senses. By staying present and aware, I can catch myself before I'm led astray by a momentary desire or distraction. This isn't always easy, but with practice, it becomes more natural. The more we practice self-awareness and self-control, the more we can bring our senses under control and use them to support our growth.

The Eternal Struggle: Good vs. Evil Within

Perhaps the most defining characteristic of Kali Yuga is the ongoing struggle between good and evil within each of us. This struggle is not just about external actions, but about our thoughts, intentions, and desires. In this age, the line between good and evil is often blurred, and it's easy to be led astray by negative influences, both internal and external.

The key to navigating this struggle is self-awareness. We must be vigilant in monitoring our thoughts and actions, constantly checking to see if they align with our higher values. This requires honesty and humility, as well as a willingness to confront our own weaknesses and shortcomings.

At the same time, it's important to cultivate compassion and understanding towards ourselves. We are all works in progress, and the journey of self-improvement is never easy. There will be times when we fall short, when we make mistakes, or when we are tempted by negative influences. In these moments, it's important to remember that the battle is ongoing, and that every moment offers a new opportunity to choose the path of righteousness.

Embracing the Age of Self-Reflection

Kali Yuga may be an age of darkness and ignorance, but it is also an age of profound opportunity. The challenges we face in this era are internal, and they offer us the chance to grow in ways that were not possible in previous Yugas. Through self-reflection, self-discipline, and self-awareness, we can navigate the complexities of this age and emerge stronger, wiser, and more enlightened.

As we move through Kali Yuga, let us embrace the opportunity for self-reflection. Let us take the time to look inward, to understand ourselves, and to align our lives with our highest values. By doing so, we can not only overcome the challenges of this age but also add value to our own lives and the lives of others.

This is the age we are in, and the battle within us will continue until the end of our lives. But it is a battle worth fighting, for it is through this struggle that we can truly grow, evolve, and realize our highest potential.

My Self-Reflection Process

1. Finding a Quiet Space: I start by finding a peaceful place where I won't be disturbed. This could be a quiet room, a garden, or even a secluded spot in a park. The key is to be in an environment where I can focus without distractions.

2. Setting the Mood: I often set the mood by dimming the lights or lighting a candle. Sometimes, I play soft, calming music in the background. This helps create a serene atmosphere that is conducive to introspection.

3. Mirror Talk: I stand in front of a mirror and look at myself. This isn't just about seeing my reflection; it's about connecting with myself on a deeper level. I make eye contact with myself, which helps me feel more present and engaged in the process.

4. Speaking Aloud: I begin speaking aloud, addressing myself as if I were talking to a close friend. I discuss my thoughts, feelings, and experiences. This could be about something that happened during the day, a decision I need to make, or a challenge I'm facing. Speaking aloud helps me articulate my thoughts more clearly and makes the process feel more real.

5. Engaging the Senses: I involve all five senses in the process. As I speak, I walk around, allowing my body to move freely. I listen to my own voice, feeling the vibrations in my chest and throat. This physical engagement helps ground me and makes the reflection more impactful.

6. Asking Questions: I ask myself questions to dig deeper into my thoughts and feelings. Questions like, "Why did I react that way?" or "What can I learn from this experience?" help me gain insights and understand myself better.

7. Journaling: After my mirror talk, I often sit down and write in my journal. I jot down the key points from my self-reflection, any insights I gained, and any actions I want to take. Writing helps solidify my thoughts and serves as a record I can look back on.

8. Regular Practice: I make self-reflection a regular practice, doing it daily or at least a few times a week. Consistency is key to gaining deeper insights and making meaningful progress.

9. Morning and Night Routine: I usually engage in self-reflection for 15-20 minutes in the early morning and a few minutes before sleep. The morning session helps me start the day with clarity and purpose, while the evening session allows me to review the day and prepare for the next.

10. Preparation for Key Events: Before important presentations or discussions, I use self-reflection as a rehearsal. I speak to myself about the key points I want to cover, anticipate potential questions, and practice my delivery. This helps me feel more confident and ensures that my communication is effective and well-prepared.

This process has been incredibly beneficial for me, providing clarity, insight, and a sense of peace.

Self-Reflection often leads to surprising discoveries about myself. Here are a few examples:

Uncovering Hidden Emotions

Sometimes, I realize that I'm carrying emotions I wasn't fully aware of. For instance, I might discover underlying feelings of anxiety or excitement about an upcoming event. Acknowledging these emotions helps me address them more effectively.

Recognizing Patterns

Through self-reflection, I've identified patterns in my behaviour and thought processes. For example, I might notice that I tend to procrastinate when I'm feeling overwhelmed. Recognizing these patterns allows me to take proactive steps to change them.

Gaining New Perspectives

Reflecting on past experiences often gives me new insights. I might see a situation from a different angle or understand someone else's perspective better. This helps me grow and improve my relationships.

Realizing Strengths and Weaknesses

I often discover strengths I didn't fully appreciate, like resilience or creativity. Conversely, I also become more aware of areas where I need to improve, such as patience or time management.

Finding Clarity

Self-reflection helps me clarify my goals and values. I might realize that a particular goal is more important to me than I initially thought, or that my values have shifted over time. This clarity guides my decisions and actions.

Enhancing Self-Compassion

By reflecting on my experiences, I often find that I'm more compassionate towards myself. I recognize that everyone makes mistakes and that it's okay to learn and grow from them. This self-compassion is crucial for personal development.

Discovering New Interests

Sometimes, self-reflection reveals new interests or passions. I might realize that I'm drawn to a particular hobby or field of study that I hadn't considered before. This opens up new opportunities for exploration and growth.

Improving Communication

Reflecting on my interactions with others helps me improve my communication skills. I might notice areas where I could have been clearer or more empathetic. This awareness helps me communicate more effectively in the future.

Strengthening Resilience

By reflecting on past challenges, I often discover how resilient I am. I see how I've overcome difficulties and learn from those experiences. This strengthens my confidence and ability to handle future challenges.

Deepening Self-Awareness

Overall, self-reflection deepens my self-awareness. I become more attuned to my thoughts, feelings, and behaviours. This awareness is the foundation for personal growth and development.

Self-reflection is a powerful tool for personal growth, and it often leads to surprising and valuable discoveries.

Punch line: "Look within to truly see, the path to who you're meant to be."

Value 2 - The Power of Self SWOT Analysis

As I sit here, thinking back on my life over the past 40 years, I realize that one of the most valuable things I've done is take the time to truly understand myself. Life has thrown its fair share of challenges my way, but what has helped me navigate through them is having a clear picture of who I am. One of the most effective tools I've found for this purpose is the SWOT analysis. This strategic approach has allowed me to evaluate my strengths, weaknesses, opportunities, and threats, giving me a better understanding of myself and where I want to go in life.

Why SWOT Analysis is Important

When it comes to personal growth, self-awareness is key. Understanding my strengths and weaknesses helps me recognize what I'm naturally good at and where I might need to put in some extra effort. It's like having a roadmap that guides me toward becoming the best version of myself.

Another significant benefit of a SWOT analysis is that it helps with strategic planning. By identifying the opportunities and threats around me, I can plan for the future more effectively. It's not just about reacting to what life throws at me; it's about being proactive and making choices that align with my long-term goals. This kind of planning gives me confidence because I'm not just drifting—I'm navigating my way through life with purpose.

Setting goals is another area where a SWOT analysis shines. By aligning my strengths with the opportunities I see, I can set goals that are both realistic and achievable. This clarity of purpose helps me stay focused on what truly matters, rather than getting sidetracked by things that don't contribute to my growth.

Finally, understanding my strengths and weaknesses also aids in making better decisions. When I know what I'm good at and where I struggle, I can approach decisions with a more balanced perspective. This insight allows me to leverage my strengths to their fullest potential while finding ways to address my weaknesses in a constructive manner.

My SWOT Analysis

Taking a deep dive into my personal SWOT analysis has been an enlightening experience. Here's how I've broken it down:

Strengths:

Resilience: Over the years, I've faced many challenges, but my ability to bounce back has been one of my greatest strengths. Resilience isn't about avoiding difficulties; it's about how I handle them. Every time life has knocked me down, I've found a way to get back up, stronger than before. This resilience has shaped who I am today and continues to be a driving force in my life.

Empathy: My ability to understand and connect with others has been a significant asset. Empathy allows me to build strong, meaningful relationships. It's not just about being kind; it's about truly listening to others and understanding their perspectives. This trait has enriched my life in countless ways, from personal relationships to professional interactions.

Adaptability: Life is unpredictable, and being able to adapt to changing circumstances has been crucial to my growth. Whether it's a sudden change in my career or unexpected events in my personal life, my adaptability has allowed me to navigate these changes with ease. This flexibility has been key to both my personal and professional success.

Weaknesses:

Procrastination: At times, I've struggled with procrastination, delaying important tasks and decisions. I've often found myself putting things off, thinking I'll get to them later, only to realize that time has slipped away. Recognizing this weakness has been the first step towards addressing it. I've learned that breaking tasks into smaller, manageable pieces can help me overcome the urge to procrastinate.

Impatience: I've often found myself wanting immediate results, which can lead to frustration. In a world where everything seems to move at lightning speed, it's easy to expect instant gratification. However, I've learned that some things take time, and being patient is essential. It's an ongoing journey, but I'm working on trusting the process and giving myself grace.

Self-Criticism: Being overly critical of myself has sometimes hindered my progress. I have a tendency to focus on what I could have done better, rather than celebrating my achievements. While self-improvement is important, I've realized that balancing it with self-compassion is crucial. I'm learning to be kinder to myself and to recognize that perfection is not the goal—progress is.

Opportunities:

Continuous Learning: The world is full of opportunities to learn and grow. Embracing lifelong learning has opened up new avenues for both personal and professional development. Whether it's taking a new course, reading a book, or simply staying curious about the world around me, continuous learning keeps me engaged and helps me evolve.

Networking: Building and nurturing relationships with like-minded individuals has provided valuable opportunities for collaboration and growth. I've found that surrounding myself with people who share my values and aspirations has been incredibly beneficial. These connections have not only enriched my life but also opened doors to new opportunities that I might not have discovered on my own.

Technological Advancements: Leveraging technology has allowed me to stay connected, informed, and efficient in various aspects of life. In today's digital age, technology is a powerful tool that can enhance both personal and professional endeavours. From staying in touch with loved ones to expanding my professional network, technology has been a game-changer for me.

Threats:

Complacency: The risk of becoming complacent and settling for the status quo is a constant threat. It's easy to get comfortable and stop pushing myself to achieve more. However, I've learned that growth happens outside of my comfort zone. Staying motivated and challenging myself to reach new heights is essential to avoid falling into complacency.

External Pressures: Societal expectations and external pressures can sometimes divert me from my true path. In a world that constantly tells us what we should be doing, it can be challenging to stay true to ourselves. I've found that it's important to regularly check in with myself and ensure that the choices I'm making align with my values and goals, rather than succumbing to external pressures.

Health Concerns: As I age, maintaining good health becomes increasingly important. Physical and mental well-being are the foundation of a fulfilling life. I've come to realize that taking care of my health is not just about avoiding illness; it's about living a vibrant, energetic life. Prioritizing exercise, a balanced diet, and mental health practices is essential to continue thriving.

Conclusion

Conducting a SWOT analysis of my life has been an eye-opening experience. It has provided me with a clear understanding of my strengths, weaknesses, opportunities, and threats. This self-awareness has empowered me to make informed decisions, set meaningful goals, and navigate life's challenges with confidence.

As I reflect on my journey, I encourage myself to make this analysis a regular practice. Life is constantly changing, and so am I. By taking the time to reflect on where I am and where I want to go, I can continue to grow and evolve. Understanding my strengths and weaknesses, exploring the opportunities and threats in my life, and staying true to my values are all essential to charting a path towards a fulfilling and successful future.

In the end, the power of a SWOT analysis lies not just in understanding where I stand today but in guiding me towards where I want to be tomorrow. By embracing this tool, I'm not just reacting to life—I'm actively shaping my future, one step at a time.

Punch line: "Know your might, face your fears—strength and growth come from what's clear!"

Value 3 - Everything is in Our Hands

We've talked a lot about theory, but now I want to share one of my favourite stories with you. It's a story that I often tell young professionals and students, and it holds a powerful lesson about the control we have over our lives.

In a small, quiet village, there lived a man who didn't believe in God. He was an atheist, known for his sharp mind and for always questioning things that didn't make sense to him. One day, a famous guru came to visit the village, and the atheist saw this as the perfect chance to challenge the guru and prove that his so-called wisdom was nothing more than a sham.

The atheist came up with a clever plan. He caught a small sparrow and held it gently behind his back. He then approached the guru, who was surrounded by villagers eager to hear his teachings. The atheist, confident that he would outsmart the guru, asked, "If you are truly wise and possess the powers that everyone says you have, then tell me: is the sparrow in my hand alive or dead?"

The villagers held their breath, waiting to see how the guru would respond. They knew that whatever the guru said, the atheist could prove him wrong. If the guru said the bird was alive, the atheist would crush it to death and show the lifeless bird to everyone. If the guru said the bird was dead, he would open his hands and let the sparrow fly away.

The guru looked at the atheist with calm eyes and a gentle smile. Without hesitation, he said, "My friend, whether the sparrow is alive, or dead is entirely in your hands. If I say it's alive, you can choose to crush it and prove me wrong. If I say it's dead, you can choose to release it and prove me wrong. The power to decide its fate is in your hands."

The atheist was stunned. He realized that the guru had seen right through his plan. The villagers, too, were amazed by the guru's response. In that moment, the atheist understood that the guru was not just wise, but also deeply aware of the power of choice that lies within each of us.

This story teaches us several important lessons, and I want to share them with you.

1. Responsibility and Control

The first lesson is about responsibility and control. Just as the atheist had the power to decide the fate of the sparrow, we have the power to shape our own lives. It's easy to blame other people, bad luck, or circumstances for the things that go wrong in our lives. But the truth is, we are in control of our actions and decisions. Once we realize this, we can start taking responsibility for our lives, and we can begin to improve and grow.

2. Self-Reflection

The guru's response also teaches us the importance of self-reflection. Instead of looking for answers from others or blaming them for our problems, we should look within ourselves. When we take the time to reflect on our own actions, we can better understand our strengths and weaknesses. This self-awareness allows us to make better decisions and helps us grow as individuals.

3. Wisdom and Perspective

Another lesson from the story is about wisdom and perspective. The guru didn't get caught up in the atheist's challenge. Instead, he looked beyond the immediate situation and saw the bigger picture. This kind of perspective is crucial in life. When we face challenges, it's important to stay calm and think about the broader implications. By doing so, we can navigate difficult situations with clarity and composure, just like the guru.

4. Empowerment

The story is also a powerful reminder of empowerment. It shows us that we are not helpless victims of our circumstances. Instead, we are active participants in our own destiny. When we embrace this idea, we realize that we have the power to make positive changes in our lives. We can set goals, take action, and achieve the things we want. This sense of empowerment is incredibly motivating and can drive us to reach new heights.

5. Integrity and Honesty

Finally, the guru's response highlights the importance of integrity and honesty. He could have tried to outsmart the atheist or come up with some clever trick, but instead, he gave a straightforward and truthful answer. This honesty-built trust and respect among the villagers. It's a reminder that being truthful and transparent in our actions is always the best policy. When we act with integrity, we stay true to our values and principles, and this earns us the respect of others.

How This Story Inspired Me

This story has had a profound impact on my life. It taught me that I have the power to shape my own destiny. Whenever I face challenges or feel overwhelmed by external circumstances, I remember the guru's words: "The power to determine its fate lies with you." This realization has been incredibly empowering for me.

By internalizing the lessons from this story, I've learned to stop blaming others or external factors for my problems. Instead, I focus on what I can control—my own actions and decisions. This shift in mindset has allowed me to approach life with a greater sense of responsibility and purpose.

Regular self-reflection has become a key part of my life. It helps me understand my strengths and weaknesses, which in turn allows me to make better decisions. I've learned to be more thoughtful and deliberate in my actions, and this has led to significant personal and professional growth.

In my journey towards becoming a "Valuepreneur"—someone who adds value to life and embraces every opportunity for growth—this story has been a cornerstone. It has reminded me time and again that everything is in my hands. Whether I succeed or fail, it's up to me. This sense of ownership over my life has been incredibly empowering, and it's something that I hope to pass on to others.

In conclusion, the story of the atheist and the guru is more than just a tale of wisdom; it's a powerful lesson about the control we have over our own lives. By taking responsibility for our actions, engaging in self-reflection, adopting a wise perspective, embracing our empowerment, and acting with integrity, we can shape our destiny and achieve our goals. Everything is, indeed, in our hands.

Punch line: "Everything's in our hands, we shape the lands,

With dreams as our guide, the future expands!"

Value 4 - The Power of Karma

Karma is one of those concepts that we hear about often, but it takes time to truly understand its significance. At its core, karma is the idea that our actions, whether good or bad, have consequences that will come back to us in some way, often when we least expect it. It's a powerful force that shapes our lives based on what we do. For me, karma is not just a belief; it's a guiding principle that I've come to trust deeply over the years.

Understanding Karma

Karma teaches us that everything we do has an impact, not just on others but on our own lives as well. When we perform good deeds, we attract positivity and good outcomes. Conversely, when we engage in negative actions, we invite challenges and difficulties into our lives. This is the cycle of cause and effect, a universal law that operates impartially. It doesn't matter who we are; karma treats everyone the same. What's most fascinating about karma is that it doesn't always act immediately. Sometimes, it takes time for the results of our actions to show up, but rest assured, they do.

This understanding of karma has influenced how I live my life. I strive to act with kindness and integrity, always mindful that what I do today will shape my tomorrow. It's a simple yet profound way of looking at life, one that encourages us to be our best selves.

My Real-Life Example of Karma

Let me share a personal story that truly illustrates the power of karma and the importance of forgiveness.

Several years ago, I was working at a company where I held a significant position at a relatively young age. This achievement, however, didn't sit well with some of the older, more senior employees. They saw me as a threat and began to undermine my efforts. They engaged in office politics, spreading rumours, and creating obstacles for me. It was a tough time, filled with stress and frustration. Eventually, I decided it wasn't worth the mental and emotional toll, so I left the job.

Moving on was one of the best decisions I ever made. I joined another company where I was offered an even higher position with more responsibilities. With time, I gained more experience and authority, and my career flourished. Then, an interesting twist of fate occurred. I found myself in a position where I had the power to negatively impact my previous company. I could have easily used my new influence to get back at those who had wronged me. The opportunity for revenge was right there, but I chose not to take it.

Why? Because I remembered the principles of karma. I knew that seeking revenge would only perpetuate the cycle of negativity. Instead, I decided to let go of the anger and resentment I had been holding onto. I chose forgiveness, trusting that karma would take care of the rest.

Years later, I heard that my old company was struggling. They were facing numerous challenges and were not doing well at all. One day, out of the blue, I received a call from one of the top executives of that company. He explained the difficulties they were facing and acknowledged the mistakes that had been made in the past. He even praised me for my decision to forgive and not seek revenge. He admitted that my actions had left a lasting impression on him and others in the company.

This conversation was a powerful moment for me. It reinforced my belief in karma and the importance of forgiveness. It showed me that good deeds do not go unnoticed, and that karma has a way of balancing the scales.

Key Lessons from Karma

From this experience, I learned several important lessons that continue to guide my life:

Actions Have Consequences: Karma reminds us that every action we take, whether good or bad, has consequences. This understanding encourages us to act with integrity and kindness, knowing that our deeds will shape our future. It's a reminder that we are responsible for the energy we put out into the world.

The Power of Forgiveness: Forgiving those who have wronged us is one of the most powerful things we can do. It breaks the cycle of negativity and allows us to move forward with peace in our hearts. Holding onto anger and resentment only weighs us down, but forgiveness frees us from those burdens.

Letting Go of Revenge: Seeking revenge might seem satisfying in the moment, but it ultimately perpetuates negativity. By letting go of the desire for retribution, we free ourselves from the burden of anger and resentment. This not only brings us peace but also aligns us with positive karma.

Trusting the Process: Karma works in its own time and in its own way. Sometimes, we may not see immediate results from our actions, but that doesn't mean karma isn't working. Trusting the process allows us to focus on our own growth and well-being, knowing that justice will be served in due course.

Living with Integrity: Understanding karma encourages us to live with integrity and compassion. Our actions today will shape our future, so it's essential to act in ways that align with our values and principles. This is the foundation of a life well-lived.

How This Story Inspired Me

This experience with karma and forgiveness has been a major turning point in my life. It taught me that holding onto anger and seeking revenge only harms us in the long run. By choosing to forgive and let go, I was able to move forward with a clear conscience and a positive mindset. This approach has brought me peace and allowed me to focus on my own growth and success.

Moreover, this experience has shown me that good deeds do not go unnoticed. Even when it seems like no one is watching, karma is always at work, balancing the scales in its own time. This understanding has strengthened my commitment to living with integrity and treating others with kindness and respect.

In conclusion, the power of karma is real, and it's something we should all be mindful of in our daily lives. By understanding that our actions have consequences, by choosing forgiveness over revenge, and by trusting the process, we can create a life filled with positivity and peace. Karma is a reminder that what we put out into the world will come back to us, so let's make sure it's something good.

Punch Line: Don't Kill or Murder anyone who will however commit Suicide!!!

"What you give is what you'll see, Karma's path will set you free!"

Value 5 - Life Lessons from Traffic Jams

Traffic jams are a common experience for many of us, especially in bustling cities like Bengaluru. But have you ever thought about the life lessons we can learn from these daily commutes? Let me share an interesting illustration from my own life that offers a unique perspective on how traffic jams can teach us about life. I am sure you would never hear about this logical illustration…

The Daily Commute

For six months, I drove my XUV 500 from Hebbal to Bommasandra, spending about five hours on the road each day. During these commutes, I had a quick ride mate who travelled with me to the office. We often chatted about various topics, and one day, he shared his frustration about comparing himself to a more successful friend. His friend was younger, less qualified, but earning more. My mate felt life was unfair and blamed his bad luck.

As we were stuck in slow-moving traffic, I decided to use the situation to illustrate a point. Here are the questions and scenarios I presented to him:

Why should I be behind this low-priced auto rickshaw? Does it mean he is ahead of me?

Just because someone is ahead of you in traffic doesn't mean they are better or more successful. Life is not a race where the one in front is always the winner. This taught me that everyone has their own pace and path. Being behind someone in one aspect doesn't mean they are ahead in life.

Behind our car was a huge container truck with 12 wheels, moving silently.

Sometimes, those who seem to be behind us might have more capacity and strength. We shouldn't underestimate others based on their current position. This reminded me that appearances can be deceiving, and everyone has their own strengths and capabilities.

When traffic cleared, I overtook the auto rickshaw and felt proud, but at the next signal, we were side by side again.

Life has its ups and downs. Even if we move ahead at times, we might find ourselves back at the same level as others. It's a reminder that progress is not always linear. This taught me humility and the importance of perseverance.

A high-speed car we tried to overtake took a left turn to a different destination.

Everyone has their own path and destination. Comparing ourselves to others is futile because our journeys are different. This helped me understand that we all have unique goals and timelines.

Cars started from different places at different times with different destinations.

Life is not a competition. We all have unique starting points and goals. It's important to focus on our own journey rather than comparing ourselves to others. This reinforced the idea that life is about personal growth, not competition.

Railway gates closed, and we had to wait for a slow-moving train with few passengers.

Sometimes, we face delays and obstacles that seem unfair. However, these moments teach us patience and resilience. This taught me to accept delays as part of the journey and to use the time to reflect and plan.

An over speeding car in the wrong direction caused frustration, but shouting at it was pointless.

Getting angry at things beyond our control is futile. It's better to stay calm and composed. Here in this case, I shouted loud inside my car with windows closed. Either other person could hear, but actually my drive mate was sitting next to me!! Hope those vibrations affected him rather than the other one. Feeling that I took my frustration from this exercise has no meaning.

This taught me the importance of maintaining inner peace and not letting external factors disturb my tranquillity.

In a narrow lane, I waited for careless cyclists and bikers to pass.

Sometimes, we need to compromise and let others go ahead for our own safety and peace of mind. It's a lesson in humility and patience. This taught me the value of patience and the importance of prioritizing safety over ego.

Honking horns behind me didn't make me move faster in a traffic jam.

External pressures shouldn't dictate our actions. We need to stay focused and calm, regardless of the noise around us. This taught me to stay true to my pace and not be swayed by external pressures.

An ambulance needed to pass, and everyone gave way.

There are times when we need to prioritize others' needs over our own. It's a reminder of empathy and compassion. This taught me the importance of empathy and the need to support others in critical situations.

Traffic police stopped me to check documents, slowing me down.

Sometimes, we face checks and balances that seem unnecessary but are essential for our safety and compliance. This taught me the importance of following rules and being prepared for unexpected checks.

Humps and potholes affected my car, but I adapted and improved my driving skills.

Life's obstacles can be frustrating, but they also help us grow and improve. Embracing challenges makes us stronger and more skilled. This taught me to see obstacles as opportunities for growth and improvement.

After a long wait in traffic, I felt triumphant when it cleared, only to be stopped by another red light.

Just like in life, moments of progress can be followed by unexpected stops. It's important to stay patient and persistent. This taught me that progress is often interrupted, but persistence is key.

Seeing a BMW waiting for walkers to cross, I wondered if the driver felt frustrated.

Sometimes, our ego can be challenged when we have to wait or give way. It's a lesson in humility and respecting others, regardless of their status. This taught me to respect others' rights and to manage my ego.

We see people in different types of vehicles, from cycles to luxury cars.

Everyone is at different stages in life, with varying levels of wealth, status, and education. On the road, we all share the same space and must navigate it together. This taught me the importance of coexistence and mutual respect.

I always followed traffic rules, but others often broke them.

Following the rules doesn't guarantee safety if others don't. We must be vigilant and prepared for the unexpected, focusing on our own actions. This taught me to be cautious and to take responsibility for my own safety.

Different speed limits on the same road.

Life has its own pace, with times to speed up and slow down. We need to adapt to these changes and understand that progress isn't always at full speed. This taught me to be flexible and to adjust my pace according to the situation.

Key Lessons

1. Stop Comparing: Life is not a race. Everyone has their own journey, and comparing ourselves to others only leads to frustration. Focus on your own path and progress.

2. Embrace Patience: Traffic jams teach us patience. Delays and obstacles are part of life, and learning to navigate them calmly helps us grow.

3. Stay Calm: Getting angry or frustrated at things beyond our control is pointless. Staying calm and composed allows us to handle situations better.

4. Prioritize Empathy: Sometimes, we need to prioritize others' needs over our own. Empathy and compassion make us better individuals.

5. Adapt and Improve: Life's challenges help us grow. Embrace obstacles as opportunities to improve and become more resilient.

6. Focus on Your Journey: Everyone has a unique path and destination. Focus on your own journey and goals, rather than comparing yourself to others.

Punch line: "Life's like a traffic jam, don't rush or cram.

Slow down, find your flow, you'll still reach where you go!"

Value 6 - 'Crying Baby Gets the Milk'

In my professional journey, one of the most important lessons I learned didn't come early on but thankfully arrived in time to save me from further setbacks. For the first decade of my 21-year career, I made a significant mistake: I kept my problems to myself. I believed that admitting I needed help or that I was struggling would make me appear weak or incompetent. To me, asking for assistance seemed like acknowledging failure, so I avoided it at all costs.

Instead, I focused on doing my work quietly, assuming that as long as I fulfilled my responsibilities, support would naturally come my way. I thought that if I just kept my head down and worked hard, things would fall into place. But that assumption turned out to be completely wrong. By refusing to ask for help, I often found myself stuck in difficult situations, unable to move forward when a bit of support could have made all the difference.

It wasn't until a few pivotal moments in my life that I started to see things differently. I began to notice that the people who were really advancing in their careers weren't the ones who silently endured their challenges. Instead, they were the ones who spoke up when they needed help. These weren't cries of desperation, but rather confident and clear requests for the resources and assistance necessary to succeed.

This realization hit me hard, and it changed my perspective completely: "The crying baby always gets the milk."

To understand this concept, think about a mother with five children. When it's time to feed them, does she start with the oldest and work her way down to the youngest? No, she feeds the child who cries first. It doesn't matter which child is the oldest or who has waited the longest; the one who makes their needs known gets attention first. This isn't about fairness or order—it's about making sure your needs are recognized.

Once I understood this, I began to apply it to my own life and career. I realized that if I wanted to grow and move forward, I couldn't afford to stay silent. I needed to speak up, ask for help when I needed it, and make sure that others knew what I required to succeed.

In the professional world, those who ask for help are often the ones who get it. The realization that I had been holding myself back simply by not asking for help was eye-opening. I had spent years struggling in silence, believing that this was the right way to handle things, when in reality, it was only keeping me from progressing.

After this realization, everything changed for me. I no longer hesitated to speak up when I needed something. I made sure that my voice was heard whether it was about needing more resources for a project, seeking advice from a colleague, or simply asking for clarification on a task. I understood that if I didn't speak up, I might be left waiting while someone else received the help I needed.

This new approach was a game-changer. My career began to progress more smoothly because I wasn't afraid to ask for what I needed. I wasn't stuck in the same old patterns of struggle and frustration. Instead, I was moving forward, receiving the support and resources that helped me perform better and achieve my goals.

Looking back, I can see how much I missed out on during those first ten years by not asking for help. I thought I was being strong by not admitting to my struggles, but in reality, I was just making things harder for myself. Now, I understand that asking for help isn't a sign of weakness—it's a sign of wisdom. It shows that you're aware of your limits and that you're committed to finding solutions rather than getting stuck in problems.

So, if there's one piece of advice, I could give to anyone, it's this: Don't be afraid to ask for help. Whether it's in your personal life or your career, speaking up about your needs is crucial. The people who get ahead are not necessarily the ones who can do it all on their own, but the ones who know when to ask for assistance.

In the end, it all comes down to this simple truth: The crying baby gets the milk. If you want to get what you need, you have to make your voice heard. Don't wait in silence, hoping that someone will notice your struggles. Speak up, ask for what you need, and you'll be far more likely to receive the support that will help you succeed.

This lesson has had a profound impact on my life, and it's one that I carry with me every day. I'm no longer afraid to ask for help, and as a result, I've been able to achieve more than I ever thought possible. So, the next time you find yourself struggling, remember: It's okay to be the crying baby. Because in the end, the one who cries out is the one who gets the milk.

Punch line: "Baby's tears, milk's near—cry no more, the bottle's here!"

Value 7 - Mr. Lucky! How I Grabbed My First Job... The Power of Luck and Humour

Sometimes in life, things happen that we can't explain. We call it luck, fate, or destiny. But what if I told you that luck, combined with a good sense of humour, can change the course of your life? That's exactly what happened to me when I landed my first job. Let me take you back to that day when a mix of luck and humour kick-started my professional journey and led me to become a "Valuepreneur"

The Start of My Job Hunt

It was my last semester of engineering, a time when the excitement of finishing college was mixed with the anxiety of what would come next. Our college had a great reputation, so many companies came to hire fresh talent. This was the placement season—a time when all students, including me, would dress up in our best clothes, clutching our resumes, and head off to face one company after another.

At first, I participated with a lot of enthusiasm. Every time a company came to our campus, I was there, ready to give it my best shot. But as the days went by, and after several rejections, my enthusiasm began to fade. I wasn't the only one feeling this way. Many of us were losing hope after being rejected repeatedly. The atmosphere among the students was becoming increasingly tense, with fewer smiles and more nervous looks.

The Golden Opportunity

Weeks went by, and one day, we received a special announcement. A top automotive company was coming to our campus to hire fresh graduates for their new factory. This wasn't just any company; it was one of the biggest names in the industry. Our placement officer was very excited and kept saying this was a golden opportunity—probably one of the last big opportunities of the year.

But after so many rejections, I wasn't as excited as I should have been. Still, with some encouragement from friends and the thought of this being one of the last chances, I decided to participate.

The First Round

The first round of selection was a written test. I gave it my best, though my confidence wasn't as high as it had been earlier in the placement season. When the results came out, I was ranked 8th out of 10. This was a bit of a relief, as it meant I had at least cleared the first hurdle.

Here's where things got interesting. The top two candidates in the written exam were directly selected, and there were three positions available. That meant they needed to pick one more person from the ranks of 3 to 10, and the final selection would be based on a personal interview. This made me nervous, as I wasn't sure how I would perform in the interview, especially given how low my confidence was at that point.

The Nerve-Wracking Interview Process

The final round was a personal interview with two gentlemen who I would never forget. One was from the sister company where the new factory was coming up, and the other was the Human Resource head of the parent company—a man of considerable influence.

The first candidate, who was ranked 1st, went into the interview room with a lot of tension, even though he didn't know he was already selected. He spent about 20 minutes inside and came out looking a bit relieved. Naturally, the rest of us were curious, so we crowded around him, asking about the questions he was asked. He said they focused heavily on Thermodynamics. Hearing this, everyone quickly pulled out their Thermodynamics books and began cramming.

Then it was the turn of the 2nd-ranked candidate. He walked in and came out after 15 minutes, looking joyful. He told us that they asked him about his favourite subject, and the questions were entirely based on that. This brought a sigh of relief among the rest of us. The tension eased, and people started flipping through their favourite subjects, hoping to be asked similar questions.

The interviews went on, and by the time the 6th candidate came out, it was apparent that they had selected him for the third and final position, although we didn't know this at the time.

My Turn - The Twist of Fate

Finally, it was my turn. I was nervous but determined. As soon as the 7th candidate came out, I rushed inside the room, eager to make a good impression. I greeted them enthusiastically, but to my surprise, they seemed a bit disinterested. They asked me to wait outside for a while until they called me back.

After what felt like an eternity, I heard someone call out from inside. I quickly rushed back in, but instead of being greeted with questions, I got a shock. The interviewers looked upset. One of them said they had actually called for someone to bring them tea and asked me to step outside again. Embarrassed, I left the room, feeling like I had just blown my chance.

As I stood outside, feeling dejected, our placement officer entered the room. I'm not sure what he said, but I think he must have requested them to complete the interviews to keep our spirits up. After a few minutes, I was called back inside.

The Game-Changer - Luck and Humour

This time, I entered with more enthusiasm, determined to make the most of whatever time I had left. The first question they asked was why I had entered the room earlier without permission, which had confused them.

Now, this was the moment that would change everything. Without missing a beat, I replied, "I was so enthusiastic about joining such a reputed automotive company that I was very sensitive to any information and rushed in with excitement."

My answer made one of them smile, and the atmosphere in the room shifted. I could feel the tension easing, and I knew I had their attention.

Just as the interview was getting started, their tea arrived. One of the interviewers remarked to the other that tea was the best option during breaks. Seizing the opportunity, I casually mentioned, “In Karnataka, coffee is actually very famous and healthier than tea. Coffee even originated in Karnataka at Baba Budangiri hills, Chikmagalur. It’s our own native crop, and so it’s quite unique.”

This little piece of trivia caught their interest. One of them was amused and asked the waiter to bring coffee instead, just to try it. This light-hearted exchange made them feel more comfortable with me, and I could tell that the interview was going in the right direction.

The Million Dollar Question

After a few more questions about various topics, which I answered confidently, the moment of truth arrived. One of the interviewers handed me a pen and a piece of paper and asked me to draw the engineering symbol for a turbine. I paused for a moment and then drew the symbol.

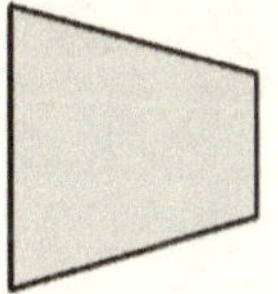

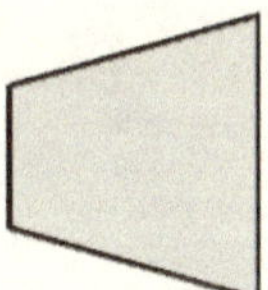

First one is actually symbol of compressor, but I wrote as turbine. Second one is actually correct symbol of turbine.

As I was drawing, I noticed that one of the interviewers looked disappointed. He asked me if I was sure, it was the correct symbol. Although I had seen his reaction, I had no choice but to say, “Yes, I’m confident.”

That’s when he dropped the bombshell. He said, “That’s the wrong answer. You’ve drawn the symbol for a compressor, which is just the opposite horizontal flip version of a turbine!”

The Turning Point

This was the critical moment—the turning point of my professional life. What I said next would determine my future.

I took a deep breath and replied, "Dear sir, I drew the symbol from *your* point of view. So, it looks opposite to me."

For a moment, there was silence. Then, the interviewer who had been smiling earlier burst out laughing. The other one, who had been serious until then, also started to laugh. They were clearly impressed by my quick thinking and humour.

And that was it. I was selected.

But here's the twist: I wasn't selected for the position at the sister company's new factory. The HR head from the parent company, who was so impressed with my responses, decided that I would be a better fit for their main operations. He saw potential in me, believing that I had what it took to excel at the parent company.

The Start of My Journey

That's how luck and a good sense of humour kick-started my professional journey. I was chosen for a position at one of the most prestigious companies in the industry, not just because of my technical knowledge, but because I could think on my feet and bring a sense of humour to the table.

Looking back, I realize that this was a pivotal moment in my life. It taught me that while knowledge and skills are important, so are attitude, confidence, and the ability to connect with people. Sometimes, it's the little things—like a well-timed joke or a piece of trivia—that can make all the difference.

This experience also taught me the power of staying positive, even when things seem to be going wrong. It's easy to get discouraged after rejections or setbacks, but it's important to keep going, to stay hopeful, and to find humour in the situation. You never know when your big break is just around the corner.

That day marked the beginning of my journey toward becoming a Valuepreneur—someone who adds value to every aspect of life, both personally and professionally. And it all started with a bit of luck, a sense of humour, and the ability to turn a mistake into an opportunity.

Punch line: "With luck on your side and humour so bright, life's a grand stage where you shine with delight!"

Value 8 - My Belief in GOD

From a very young age, I found myself drawn to the divine in ways that most children probably wouldn't comprehend. At the age of five, my fascination with godly idols was not limited to their beauty or their presence on the altar at home. I took them beyond the confines of our house, into the dirt and the mud, where I played with them as if they were my closest companions. My parents would watch in both amusement and curiosity as I carried these idols to the road, letting them partake in my childlike adventures, soaked in water and earth. Perhaps it was unusual, but even then, I sensed that these idols represented something much more profound than mere clay figures—they were symbols of a presence I couldn't yet articulate.

As I grew older, this connection deepened, influenced heavily by the television serials that dominated Indian households in the late 1980s and early 1990s. Shows like *Ramayan* and *Mahabharat* weren't just entertainment; they were weekly sermons that instilled in me a set of values and a deeper understanding of the human condition. These epic tales of gods, heroes, and moral dilemmas painted vivid pictures in my young mind, shaping my thoughts on good, evil, and the divine. The rituals, the battles, the dharma—all of it contributed to a growing sense of reverence and a belief system that, even at that young age, felt incredibly significant.

Year after year, my understanding of GOD evolved. What began as a simple acceptance of tales and traditions transformed into a mature belief system, one that, at the age of 40, I can confidently say I have fully embraced. But my journey with faith wasn't without its questions. The diversity of belief systems around the world, particularly within Sanatana Dharma itself, sometimes left me wondering. If there is one true GOD, why are there so many different names, forms, and practices? Why do some people worship Vishnu, while others revere Shiva, and yet others, Allah, or Jesus?

The answer, I eventually realized, lies in the diversity of human experience. I like to compare it to the mobile networks we use today. Take Airtel, for example—a large network in India. You might wonder, why doesn't every Indian subscribe to Airtel? Why do some people prefer Jio, Vodafone, or BSNL? Similarly, why don't we all drive the same car or wear the same brand of clothing, even if the price, quality, and durability are comparable? The answer is simple: human beings are unique, with different needs, preferences, and circumstances. Our choices in life, whether mundane or spiritual, are reflections of this uniqueness.

This realization led me to understand that the multiplicity of gods and religions is not a contradiction, but rather a celebration of diversity. Just as every network has its own coverage areas and strengths, every belief system offers its own path to the divine. What matters is not the name or form of the god we worship, but the sincerity and depth of our faith.

My spiritual journey often takes me to temples across South India, places that I visit every six months. These temples, to me, are like the network towers of the divine. Just as our phones search for the strongest signal, I believe that my soul seeks the positive energy emitted by these sacred places. Temples are not merely structures of stone and metal; they are powerhouses of spiritual energy, strategically placed to connect us with the divine. When I enter the temple's range, I feel a palpable shift—a surge of positivity that rejuvenates my mind and body.

For me, the act of visiting a temple is not about asking for specific blessings—money, success, health, or happiness. It is about tuning in to the divine frequency, receiving the positive vibes that I believe are continuously broadcasted from these holy places. Who knows, perhaps if I asked for less, GOD might have given me more. But I don't believe in bargaining with the divine. Instead, I trust that GOD, in his infinite wisdom, knows exactly what I need—what, when, who, why, where, and how to guide me towards excellence.

Finally, I've come to understand that GOD is not necessarily the grand, otherworldly figure depicted in art and media. He might not appear in the thunderous clouds or in a radiant glow. Instead, GOD could be the ordinary person standing next to you in the crowd, the stranger who helps you in a moment of need, or the friend who offers words of comfort when you least expect it. Miracles, I've learned, don't always announce themselves with fanfare; sometimes they come quietly, in the form of kindness and love.

In essence, my belief in GOD is rooted in a deep understanding that the divine is both within and around us, manifesting in ways we might not always recognize. As I continue this journey, I find myself ever more grateful for the faith that has carried me through life's ups and downs, a faith that grows stronger with each passing day.

Punch line: "Luck and humour pave the way, turning every setback into a brighter day!"

Value 9- Decoding GOD

There was a time in my life when my relationship with God was a source of deep frustration and disappointment. I would pray with all my heart, sending my hopes and wishes up to the heavens, hoping for some kind of response, some sign that my prayers were heard. But all too often, I was met with silence. When the things I asked for didn't happen, I would feel crushed, wondering why my prayers seemed to go unanswered. This led to a sense of disillusionment. Sometimes, I would even stop praying altogether, feeling like my faith was pointless. In those younger days, I believed that praying was like a transaction—a simple exchange where I would offer my devotion and, in return, God would bless me with what I desired. But as time went on, life began to teach me that this understanding was far too simplistic.

One day, during one of my regular visits to a temple, I experienced a moment of clarity that changed the way I viewed my relationship with God. It was an ordinary day, but the thought that crossed my mind was anything but ordinary. As I stood at the entrance of the temple, my eyes fell upon a menu card displayed near the donation counter. This menu card listed various sevas or offerings that devotees could make to the deity. These offerings ranged from simple rituals that cost 20 INR to more elaborate and expensive ones that could cost as much as 5000 INR. There were also options for special or VIP darshans (viewings of the deity), which required a fee, while regular darshans were free of charge but often required a longer wait.

As I looked at this menu card, I began to wonder why people approached God in such different ways. Why did some people wait patiently in long lines for a free darshan, while others chose to pay for a quicker, more exclusive experience? Why did some offer simple, modest sevas, while others spent large sums of money on more elaborate rituals? This observation made me realize something profound: these different approaches weren't just about differences in wealth or convenience. They were symbolic of the diverse ways that people seek to connect with God.

In that moment, it dawned on me that there isn't just one correct way to reach God. Every person's journey is unique, shaped by their individual circumstances, beliefs, and desires. Some people find their connection to God through quiet, humble acts of devotion, while others might feel closer to the divine through grand, elaborate rituals. The path each person takes is less important than the dedication and persistence with which they follow it. What truly matters is that we don't give up—that we continue to seek God, even when it feels like our prayers are not being answered.

This period of reflection also brought clarity to another question that had puzzled me for a long time: Why does Sanatana Dharma have so many gods? Why do we worship so many different forms of the divine? The answer, I realized, is similar to something we see in everyday life, especially in large organizations.

In any big company, while the CEO is the ultimate authority, there are also various department heads—chiefs of Finance, Operations, Human Resources, and so on. Each of these chiefs has a specific role and is responsible for managing their particular area of the business based on their expertise. Similarly, in the realm of the divine, each god or goddess in Sanatana Dharma represents a different aspect of the divine, each one overseeing a specific function in the universe. Just as a company needs different leaders to function smoothly, the universe requires different manifestations of the divine to maintain harmony and order.

This realization brought me a deep sense of peace. I began to see that just as each department in a company plays an important role, each god and goddess in Sanatana Dharma serves an essential purpose in the grand scheme of things. They are not separate entities, but different expressions of the same divine force, each one necessary for the balance and functioning of the cosmos.

As I continued to reflect on my spiritual journey, I understood that my earlier frustrations with prayer and faith stemmed from a limited perspective. I had viewed my relationship with God as a simple give-and-take, where I expected immediate results in exchange for my devotion. But life had more to teach me. I learned that the path to God is not about receiving everything we ask for, but about growing in understanding, patience, and trust.

Over time, I came to see that faith is not a straightforward transaction; it's a journey filled with moments of doubt, discovery, and sometimes disappointment. But it's through these experiences that we grow closer to the divine. The silence I once feared in my prayers was not an absence of God, but rather an invitation to look deeper, to find meaning beyond my immediate desires.

In the end, I realized that the path to God is as varied and diverse as the people who walk it. There is no single method, no one-size-fits-all approach. What truly matters is that we keep seeking, keep believing, and keep walking our path with faith and hope in our hearts. Whether through simple prayers, elaborate rituals, or quiet reflection, every sincere effort to connect with the divine is valid and meaningful.

This understanding transformed my relationship with God. I no longer saw unanswered prayers as failures but as opportunities for growth and learning. I began to appreciate the wisdom in the silence and to trust that, even when I didn't receive what I asked for, God was still guiding me on the path that was best for me. This shift in perspective brought a sense of peace and acceptance that I had long been searching for.

Looking back, I can see that my spiritual journey was never really about getting what I wanted from God. It was about learning to trust in the process, to have faith even when the path was unclear, and to understand that every step, whether easy or difficult, was leading me closer to a deeper, more meaningful connection with the divine.

In conclusion, my relationship with God has evolved from one of frustration and unmet expectations to one of trust, understanding, and peace. I've come to see that the path to the divine is not about the specific steps we take, but about the intention and sincerity with which we walk our path. And as long as we keep moving forward with faith and hope, we are never truly lost.

Punch Line : "Decode the Divine, Where Faith and Reason Align!"

Value 10 - The Borewell Story - A Lesson in Focus, Dedication, and Mastering Your Niche

Yes, you heard it right—this is the Borewell Story. It's not just a story about drilling for water; it's a story that teaches us about focus, dedication, and the importance of mastering our niche. These are words we often hear in motivational talks, but they can sometimes feel abstract or hard to relate to. That's why I think this story explains them in a much more relatable and practical way.

This conversation happened during one of my regular carpool rides from home to the office. The journey usually takes around two hours one way, giving us plenty of time to chat about various things. On this particular day, one of my carpool buddies was talking about working smart and multitasking. He shared an experience that had been bothering him for a while.

He works in a fast-paced office environment, where it seems like everyone around him is juggling multiple tasks and still managing to climb the corporate ladder faster than him. He was puzzled and frustrated. He said, "I see my colleagues doing several things at once, and even though they don't seem to finish anything 100%, they're still moving ahead in their careers. I tried to do the same, but I couldn't make it work. Instead of getting ahead, I just ended up feeling overwhelmed and unproductive."

His frustration was clear. He had been trying to emulate his colleagues' approach, thinking that multitasking was the key to success. But for him, it didn't seem to work. That's when I remembered the Borewell process I had gone through at home the previous week, and it struck me that it could be a perfect analogy for this situation.

Let me explain.

Last week, I decided to have a borewell drilled at my house. The process was fascinating and taught me a lot about focus and dedication. When I spoke to the geologist, he predicted that the water source would be available at around 1,000 feet below the ground. Now, drilling a borewell isn't just about digging a random hole and hoping for the best. It requires precision, patience, and persistence. The goal is clear—you need to reach the water source, and to do that, you have to drill deep enough, without getting distracted by other things.

As the drilling process began, I watched the workers operate the heavy machinery. The drill started slowly, inching its way into the ground. The first few feet were relatively easy; the soil was soft, and the drill moved quickly. But as we went deeper, the resistance increased. The ground became harder, and the progress slowed down. Yet, the workers didn't give up. They kept the drill steady, focusing all their efforts on reaching that 1,000-foot mark.

At around 800 feet, we hit a rocky layer. The drill struggled to penetrate the rock, and the progress almost came to a halt. This was the critical point. We could have given up or tried to drill in a different direction, but that would have been counterproductive. The water source was straight down, not sideways. So, the workers adjusted the drill bit, applied more pressure, and kept going. It was tough, and it took time, but eventually, they broke through the rock and reached the water at around 1,020 feet.

The sense of achievement was immense. We had focused on one goal, dedicated our efforts, and mastered the process. And in the end, it paid off. We struck water, just as the geologist had predicted. Meanwhile, I was also thinking earlier that can I dig 100 feet each to sum up of 1000 feet and get water at 10 places? So strange thinking, right? It took time for me to realise a true learning out of it.

As I watched the water gush out from the borewell, it hit me—this is exactly how we should approach our work and our careers. In today's fast-paced world, there's a lot of pressure to do everything at once, to multitask, and to keep up with everyone else. But that's not always the best approach. Just like drilling a borewell, success in any field requires focus, dedication, and the patience to master your niche.

When you try to do too many things at once, you end up spreading yourself too thin. You might feel busy, but you're not really making progress. You're not going deep enough to reach the "water"—the success and fulfilment that come from truly mastering something.

Let's take a closer look at what happened during the Borewell process and how it relates to our work lives.

Focus on a Single Goal

In the Borewell story, the goal was clear: reach the water source, which was 1,000 feet below the ground. There was no confusion, no distractions, and no side projects. The workers had one job—to drill down to that depth. If they had tried to dig in multiple places or changed directions every time they hit a tough spot, they would have never reached the water.

The same goes for your career. When you focus on a single goal or a specific area of expertise, you're more likely to succeed. It's about going deep, not wide. Instead of trying to be good at many things, try to be excellent at one thing. This is where true mastery comes from. It's not about how many things you can juggle; it's about how well you can perform the task at hand.

Dedication and Persistence

The drilling process wasn't easy. The workers faced challenges, especially when they hit the rocky layer at 800 feet. But they didn't give up. They knew the water was there, and they were dedicated to reaching it. This required persistence, patience, and a lot of hard work. But in the end, their dedication paid off.

In our work lives, we often face obstacles and challenges. It's easy to get discouraged and think about giving up or switching to something easier. But if you're dedicated to your goal and persistent in your efforts, you'll eventually break through those obstacles. Success doesn't come overnight; it's the result of consistent effort over time.

Mastering Your Niche

Finally, the Borewell story teaches us about the importance of mastering your niche. The workers were skilled in operating the drill. They knew exactly what to do when they encountered different types of soil and rock. They had the expertise to adjust the drill bit, apply the right amount of pressure, and keep the drill on course. This mastery of their craft was crucial to their success.

In your career, mastering your niche is just as important. Whatever field you're in, take the time to learn and develop your skills. Become an expert in your area of work. When you're truly skilled at something, you'll find that opportunities start to come your way. People will recognize your expertise, and you'll stand out from the crowd.

After sharing the Borewell story with my carpool buddy, he had a moment of realization. He understood that while multitasking might work for some people, it wasn't the right approach for him. Instead, he decided to focus on what he was truly good at and dedicate himself to mastering that skill. He realized that by focusing on one goal and putting in the necessary effort, he could achieve much more than by trying to do everything at once.

The Borewell story is a simple yet powerful reminder that focus, dedication, and mastering your niche are the keys to success. It's not about how much you do, but how well you do it. So, the next time you feel overwhelmed by the pressure to multitask or keep up with others, remember the Borewell. Focus on your goal, dedicate yourself to it, and keep drilling until you reach the water.

Punch line: "Dig deep, stay true, success will come to you!"

Value 11- Find Your GURU—How and Why?

In today's world, the word "Guru" has expanded far beyond its original Sanskrit roots. It has become a universally recognized term, synonymous with a guide, a teacher, or a mentor. In India, calling someone a Guru is almost instinctive when we refer to those who teach us, mentor us, or lead us in some way. But for the longest time, I wrestled with a question: How does one find a Guru, and why is having a Guru so important in the first place?

The answer didn't come to me quickly. It took many years and a lot of introspection before I began to understand the significance of a Guru. And surprisingly, the moment of realization came to me in the most unexpected way—through the use of Google Maps.

Yes, you read that correctly—Google Maps.

When Google Maps first came out, I was utterly fascinated by it. The idea that a small device in my hand could tell me how to navigate to any location was mesmerizing. I would use Google Maps even for routes I was already familiar with, like the drive back to my own home. There was something almost magical about watching the little blue dot move along the map, guiding me every step of the way. It seemed like such a simple pleasure at the time, but it got me thinking about how we navigate the much larger, more complex journey of life.

One day, while driving with a friend, our conversation drifted towards spirituality. My friend began talking about Sadhguru Jaggi Vasudev, a spiritual leader whom he greatly admired after visiting his Isha Ashram in Coimbatore. I saw this as the perfect chance to ask him about his experiences with having a Guru. His response was both immediate and unexpected.

He said, "A Guru is like a GPS."

At first, I was confused. I thought he was talking about the Global Positioning System, the technology behind Google Maps. But he quickly corrected me, saying, "No, I mean the Guru Positioning System."

He went on to explain that just as we rely on Google Maps to guide us through unfamiliar roads, a Guru is essential for navigating the unknown territories of life. This analogy instantly resonated with me. It made perfect sense, and later that day, I found myself watching a video where Sadhguru elaborated on this very concept. That video shifted my perspective on what a Guru is and why having one can be so crucial.

Consider this: when we're driving in a place we've never been before, we place our trust in Google Maps. We believe that it will show us the correct path, guide us through each turn, and even alert us if we're going too fast or too slow. The GPS becomes our silent, trustworthy companion, ensuring that we reach our destination safely. Similarly, in life's journey—full of its own set of challenges, twists, and turns—a Guru acts as our guide. A Guru helps us navigate the path to our goals, offers wisdom in times of confusion, and mentors us through difficult decisions.

Reflecting on this, I was reminded of a book I had read back in the 8th grade. It was a biography of Swami Vivekananda and his Guru, Shri Ramakrishna Paramahamsa. At the time, I didn't fully understand the depth of their relationship, but I was captivated by the stories of their conversations. One story, in particular, left a lasting impression on me.

In his early years, Swami Vivekananda, who was then known as Narendra, found it difficult to concentrate during meditation. Frustrated, he sought help from his Guru, Shri Ramakrishna. Instead of giving him a long lecture, Shri Ramakrishna simply took a small stone and lightly tapped the centre of Narendra's forehead, instructing him to focus on that point of sensation. This simple act of focused attention became a turning point for Narendra. Over time, it helped transform him into Swami Vivekananda, a towering figure in spirituality who continues to inspire millions around the world.

This story illustrates the profound impact a Guru can have. A Guru doesn't just point out the way; they help you sharpen your focus, guide you through your struggles, and support you in overcoming your doubts until you emerge stronger and wiser.

So, how do you find your Guru? The answer is not in actively searching for one, but rather in being open to guidance. Your Guru may not necessarily be a person in the traditional sense. It could be a book that resonates deeply with you, an experience that changes your perspective, or even a moment of clarity that steers you in the right direction. The key is to remain open and receptive to these moments of guidance.

And why is it important to have a Guru? Because life is a journey filled with uncertainties, challenges, and complex decisions. Having a wise guide by your side can mean the difference between wandering aimlessly and finding a clear path towards your true potential. A Guru helps you stay on course, provides you with wisdom when you're lost, and encourages you to reach for goals you never thought possible.

In many ways, finding a Guru is like discovering your own inner GPS. It's a system that helps you navigate the complexities of life, leading you to your destination with a sense of clarity and purpose. Whether you realize it or not, the guidance of a Guru—be it through a person, a book, or an experience—can have a transformative impact on your life.

To summarize, the concept of a Guru is timeless, yet it adapts to the context of modern life. Whether through ancient wisdom or modern technology, the role of a Guru remains vital in helping us find our way. Just as Google Maps guides us on the roads, a Guru guides us on the journey of life, ensuring we don't lose our way and reach our destination, whatever it may be.

Punch line: "Let your Guru be your guide, on life's wild ride, side by side."

Value 12 - The Role of the Guru and the Power of Self-Performance:

I've often found myself reflecting on a question that may seem simple on the surface but holds profound implications: Who plays the most important role when it comes to achieving results? The mentor, or the individual performing the task? This thought has lingered with me for years, growing more complex with time.

It's undeniable that a guru or mentor plays an essential role in shaping one's path. A guru provides guidance, direction, and wisdom that we might otherwise overlook. However, as crucial as a guru is, there's an element of personal responsibility that can't be ignored. The actual results, the fruits of the labour, lie in our own hands. No matter how great a teacher is, it's ultimately up to the student to take action and perform.

For instance, I often think about the world of cricket, a sport I deeply admire. When you look at someone like Virat Kohli, a player who has broken countless records, you can't help but be impressed. But then the question arises: Is Kohli's success more a result of his own talent and hard work, or the coaching and mentorship he received? Should the credit go to Virat Kohli, or should we be praising his coach, who gave him direction and honed his skills?

The same thought crosses my mind when I think about the film industry. Who deserves the most recognition in a movie—the actor who brings the character to life on screen, or the director who carefully Molds the actor's performance? An actor like

Leonardo DiCaprio or Amitabh Bachchan may deliver breathtaking performances, but could they have done it without the vision of a director guiding them? Does the Best Actor Award belong to the actor alone, or is the director equally deserving of the credit for extracting that level of performance?

These questions have fascinated me for a long time. I remember, during my college days, I would often wonder about teachers who prepare students for some of the toughest exams, like UPSC or IAS. These teachers possess a deep understanding of the subjects they teach. They know the content backward and forward, often better than their students. But here's the paradox: Despite their vast knowledge, why aren't these teachers the ones becoming the top IAS officers themselves? Why aren't they the CEOs of major corporations when they seem to have all the answers?

In a similar vein, I used to ask myself, "If a teacher knows every subject so thoroughly, why doesn't he or she score a perfect 100 in every exam?" The more I thought about it, the clearer the answer became.

It's not just about knowing; it's about doing. The best teacher or mentor can guide you, give you the tools, and show you the path. But no matter how wise or skilled they are, the final responsibility to perform lies with the individual. A coach doesn't go out on the field and score the centuries—the player does. A director doesn't stand in front of the camera and deliver lines—the actor does. And a teacher doesn't sit in the exam hall to take the test—the student does.

This realization was eye-opening for me. I began to understand that it's not enough to have a great mentor or teacher. The real challenge lies in using their guidance to surpass them; to exceed the expectations they have for you. In fact, the ultimate tribute to a great teacher or mentor is to outperform them. It's not about competing with them, but about realizing that they've given you all the tools you need to become even better.

I also came to appreciate that everyone has their role. A teacher's role isn't necessarily to become the top performer in the field—they have chosen to guide others, to share their knowledge and help others succeed. That, in itself, is a tremendous achievement. Similarly, a coach or director might not be the star on the stage or the field, but without them, the star might never have reached their full potential. There's a kind of quiet, selfless greatness in being the one who helps others shine.

But even with the best support system in place, personal effort is the key to success. You can have the world's best teacher, but unless you put in the hard work, the discipline, and the dedication, you'll never reach the heights that you're capable of. In the end, success is a combination of having great guidance and putting in your own personal effort.

Over time, I've learned that it's important to be grateful for the mentors in our lives—those who give us direction and help shape our paths. But at the same time, we must recognize our own responsibility in achieving success. We can't rely solely on someone else's knowledge or wisdom. We have to take what we've learned, apply it, and strive to go even further.

As I reflect on this, I realize that the balance between a guru's guidance and individual effort is what truly leads to success. A great mentor can open doors, but it's up to us to walk through them. And when we do, we not only honour our mentor but also fulfil our own potential.

In the end, it's not about choosing between the guru and the individual. It's about understanding that both are essential—but the final performance, the actual results, will always rest in our hands.

Punch Line: "Guidance Lights the Way, But It's Your Hands That Win the Day!"

Value 13 - The Power of Maturity – How I manage OVER SMARTEES!!!

Throughout my career, I've often encountered individuals who seem to overestimate their capabilities. These are the people who show off, always trying to prove that they are the only ones working hard, the only ones who know the right way to do things. While I've come to appreciate a certain level of confidence and even admire those who push boundaries, I've learned that there's a difference between genuine competence and the kind of overconfidence that stems from a lack of knowledge or experience.

Early in my career, dealing with these individuals was a significant challenge for me. Their overconfidence often led to unnecessary conflicts and disrupted the harmony of the workplace. At times, I found myself entangled in arguments, trying to assert my own experience and knowledge against their baseless claims. This approach, however, rarely led to a positive outcome. Instead, it often resulted in frustration and wasted time. It wasn't until I heard a story from one of my mentors that I gained a new perspective on how to handle such situations.

The story my mentor shared with me has stayed with me ever since. It's a simple tale, but its lesson is profound. It goes like this:

In a jungle, there was once a fierce argument between a tiger and an overconfident fox. The fox, known for its cunning and cleverness, claimed that it was the most intelligent animal in the jungle. With its sharp wit, the fox boasted that it could even kill the mighty tiger. The tiger, known for its strength and power, was enraged by the fox's audacity. How could a small fox dare to challenge a tiger? The tiger defended itself, arguing that while cleverness is important, strength is equally necessary.

The argument escalated to the point where many other animals and birds gathered to watch. It became such a spectacle that they all decided to take the matter to the lion, the king of the jungle. The lion listened patiently as the tiger and the fox presented their cases. The tiger was serious, genuinely believing that the fox needed to be put in its place. The lion then turned to the tiger and asked if he was truly serious about this matter. The tiger, still fuming, confirmed that he was.

After a moment of thought, the lion delivered its verdict. "Yes," the lion said, "the fox is indeed the cleverest animal in the jungle. If it decides, it can kill even the tiger." The fox, beaming with pride, felt victorious. It strutted away, proud of the lion's words and the respect it believed it had earned from the other animals.

The tiger, however, was left feeling frustrated and disappointed. How could the lion, the king of the jungle, side with the fox? After the crowd dispersed, the tiger approached the lion and asked why it had said such a thing. The lion, with a stern expression, replied, "I am disappointed in you, tiger. You are strong, powerful, and the future king of this jungle. Yet, you allowed yourself to be drawn into an argument with a fox. A fox that, in reality, poses no threat to you. Instead of using your strength and power to deal with the situation, you wasted your time and energy arguing with a creature far beneath you. You even brought this argument to me, as if the fox was a real challenge to your authority."

The lion's words hit the tiger hard. The tiger realized that it had indeed wasted its time and energy on something that didn't deserve its attention. It was a lesson in understanding one's own strength and the futility of engaging with those who seek to undermine it without merit.

This story served as an eye-opener for me, both professionally and personally. It taught me a valuable lesson about maturity, particularly in how we deal with people who are overconfident without cause. In any environment, whether at work or in our personal lives, we will encounter individuals who, like the fox, believe they are cleverer than everyone else. They may not have the experience or knowledge to back up their claims, but their overconfidence drives them to seek recognition and assert dominance.

In the past, I might have responded to such individuals with frustration, trying to prove them wrong or show them up. But as the lion's lesson illustrates, this approach is not only futile but also beneath someone who is truly confident in their abilities. Maturity, I've learned, is about knowing when to engage and when to rise above.

When faced with such people, the best approach is often to remain calm and patient. It's important to remember that not every challenge needs to be met head-on, especially when the challenger isn't truly a threat. Engaging in arguments with those who lack knowledge or experience only serves to lower us to their level. Instead, we should focus on our own strengths and abilities, using them wisely and strategically.

In the workplace, this might mean allowing someone else to take the spotlight temporarily, even if we know they're not entirely deserving of it. Over time, true competence and experience will shine through, and those who are merely overconfident will be exposed for what they are. It's not our job to prove them wrong in the moment; our job is to continue doing our best work, confident in the knowledge that our efforts will speak for themselves.

This approach requires a high level of maturity. It's not easy to stand by and watch someone else receive undue praise or attention, especially when we know we're more deserving. But by staying calm and focused, we not only preserve our own energy but also avoid unnecessary conflicts that could detract from our productivity and overall well-being.

This lesson also extends to our personal lives. We all know people who are quick to boast or show off, often without much to back it up. Rather than getting caught up in their need for validation, it's more productive to focus on our own growth and development. By maintaining a calm and patient demeanour, we can navigate these situations without letting them affect us negatively.

Over the years, I've come to see that true maturity is about understanding our own worth and not feeling the need to constantly prove it to others. It's about recognizing that not every battle is worth fighting, and that sometimes, the best course of action is to simply walk away. This doesn't mean we're admitting defeat; rather, it means we're choosing to prioritize our own peace of mind and focus on what truly matters.

In professional settings, this mindset has helped me build stronger relationships with colleagues and create a more positive work environment. By not engaging in unnecessary conflicts, I've been able to focus on my work and contribute more effectively to my team. In turn, this has earned me respect and recognition for my skills and experience, without the need to assert myself in every situation.

Personally, this approach has brought me greater peace and satisfaction. I've learned to let go of the need to compete with others and instead focus on my own journey. This has allowed me to grow in ways that are meaningful to me, rather than constantly comparing myself to others or trying to meet external expectations.

The story of the tiger and the fox is a powerful reminder that true strength lies not in proving ourselves to others, but in knowing our own worth and staying focused on our goals. By embracing this mindset, we can navigate the challenges of life with grace and maturity, ultimately achieving greater success and fulfilment.

As I continue on my journey, I strive to embody the wisdom of the lion. I remind myself that maturity is about choosing my battles wisely, maintaining a sense of calm in the face of adversity, and always staying true to myself. This, I believe, is the key to both personal and professional growth, and the foundation of a fulfilling and successful life.

Punch line: "Rise above the chatter, let your strength be the matter."

Value 14 - Manage the Manager to succeed!

In the early years of my career, I was eager, full of ambition, and driven by the desire to succeed. Like many young professionals, I dreamed of climbing the corporate ladder, of making a name for myself, and of achieving things that would leave a lasting impact. At the time, it felt like the world was full of endless opportunities, waiting for me to make my mark.

But it wasn't until a conversation with my manager that everything started to change. It was a conversation that would set the stage for one of the most transformative periods of my life and guide me on a path I hadn't fully understood before.

It happened one afternoon, after a long and exhausting project that had consumed weeks of my time. My manager called me into his office, his usual calm expression slightly more serious than usual. He had been in the industry for over twenty years, and his rise to management was nothing short of inspiring. He had worked his way up from the ground, seeing every corner of the business and earning his position through dedication and hard work.

I sat across from him, not knowing what to expect. His calm demeanour usually meant he was about to share something important. After a moment of silence, he leaned forward and looked directly at me. "I've spent twenty years getting to where I am today," he said. "If you want to follow in my footsteps, if you want to make a real impact in this industry, you need to learn everything I do. Observe how I manage things—how I speak, how I make decisions, how I delegate tasks, and how I manage my responsibilities. If you're with me, aim to be a manager yourself within ten years. Or else, what's the point of being here?"

His words hit me like a challenge. It wasn't just a suggestion—it was a call to action. The path he was laying out wasn't going to be easy, but it was clear. If I wanted to succeed, I needed to immerse myself in everything he did and learn it all. It was daunting, but I felt a surge of determination. I knew this was my chance, and I wasn't going to waste it.

From that moment, my journey of learning and growth began. I started by observing my manager closely. I watched how he communicated with people in meetings, how he approached problems with calm confidence, and how he made decisions quickly and effectively. I paid attention to how he delegated tasks, ensuring that each team member had what they needed to succeed, and how he guided the team through difficult times with a sense of leadership that inspired confidence in all of us.

But simply watching wasn't enough. I knew I had to actively engage in the process if I wanted to grow. I began shadowing him in every opportunity I could. I attended meetings, sat in on strategy sessions, and observed how he navigated complex issues that came our way. Each interaction, every decision, and every meeting became a learning experience for me. And when I didn't understand something, I asked. I sought his feedback, eager to learn and improve.

One thing that stood out to me was his ability to remain calm under pressure. Even in the most chaotic situations, he never seemed flustered. It was as if he saw challenges as opportunities rather than obstacles. That calm composed approach became something I aspired to emulate. Over time, I found myself becoming more comfortable in difficult situations, knowing that

I had learned from someone who had mastered the art of leadership.

But this was only part of the journey. As much as I learned from my manager, I knew I had to develop my own style. His advice was invaluable, but I also needed to figure out how to apply it in a way that felt true to who I was. So, I took the initiative. I volunteered for challenging projects, knowing they would push me beyond my comfort zone. I put myself in situations where I had to lead, even when I wasn't sure if I was ready.

One particular project stands out. It was a high-stakes, time-sensitive task, and it required strong leadership to guide the team through. My manager handed it over to me, saying, "It's time for you to lead this." I felt the weight of responsibility settle on my shoulders. I knew that this was a test, a chance to prove what I had learned and show that I was capable of managing the pressures of leadership.

The project wasn't easy. There were moments when I doubted myself, moments when things didn't go as planned, and times when I felt overwhelmed. But each time, I reminded myself of what my manager had taught me. I focused on staying calm, breaking down the problems into manageable steps, and delegating tasks to the team in a way that played to their strengths.

To my surprise, I found that the more I leaned into the lessons I had learned, the more natural it felt. The team responded well to my leadership, and together we successfully completed the project. It wasn't perfect, but it was a success, and that success marked a turning point in my career. I realized that I had the ability to lead, to manage, and to make decisions. I had grown, and I was ready for more.

As the years went by, my confidence grew. I took on more responsibilities, led larger projects, and found myself contributing to strategic decisions in ways I had never imagined. My manager remained a constant source of guidance and encouragement, but it was clear that I was becoming more independent, more capable, and more confident in my abilities.

Then, as I approached the nine-year mark in my career, the day I had worked for finally arrived. I was promoted to a managerial position, just as I had hoped to achieve within ten years. The moment was surreal, and as I sat at my new desk, I reflected on the journey that had brought me here. It wasn't just about the title or the promotion—it was about the transformation I had undergone.

I had started as a young, eager professional with dreams of success, and now, I was stepping into a leadership role with confidence and experience. The journey hadn't been easy, but it had been worth it. I realized that my manager's advice all those years ago had been more than just a challenge—it had been a blueprint for success.

Looking back, I see that this experience taught me so much more than just how to become a manager. It taught me the value of mentorship, the importance of dedication, and the power of learning from those who have come before us. My manager's belief in me gave me the push I needed, but it was my commitment to learning and growing that ultimately led to my success.

Now, as I continue my career, I carry those lessons with me. I understand that success is not just about ambition but about the willingness to learn, to take on challenges, and to push beyond what we think we're capable of. I know that mentorship is a powerful force, and I am grateful for the guidance that helped shape the leader I am today.

This journey was not just about reaching a goal—it was about becoming the best version of myself, both personally and professionally. And as I look to the future, I am excited to see where this path will continue to lead me, knowing that with the right guidance and determination, anything is possible.

Punch Line: "Chase your dreams, rise and soar—your success is worth so much more!"

Value 15 - Crafting My Mission (Platinum) Statement

In the hustle and bustle of everyday life, where deadlines press down and responsibilities seem never-ending, it's easy to lose sight of why we do what we do. I had reached a point in my career where the pressure was constant, and I felt like I was running in circles, juggling one task after another with no clear direction. It was during this particularly overwhelming phase that I realized the importance of having a guiding principle—something that would ground me when everything felt chaotic. This is what led to the creation of what I now call my Platinum Statement:

"My mission in life is not merely to survive, but to thrive. To do so, with passion, some compassion, and humour in my style!"

This statement didn't just appear out of nowhere. It was the result of a journey—a process of self-reflection, conversations with mentors, and insights from friends and even strangers who shared their own philosophies. The idea started with a simple but profound question: What did I truly want from my life and my career? At first, I thought the answer would be easy, but as I began to dig deeper, I realized it was more complex than I anticipated.

Like many, my first attempt at writing a mission statement was basic and uninspiring. It went something like, "To do my best at work and make a difference." But as the years passed, I realized that this statement didn't fully capture what I wanted. Doing my best was important, of course, but I felt there was something missing—something deeper that would give my work and life more meaning and energy. I wanted to wake up each day excited, not just about the work I was doing, but about how I was doing it.

The turning point came during a long drive one weekend. I was reflecting on my career journey, thinking about all the highs and lows I had experienced. I remembered something a mentor had once told me: “Life isn’t just about reaching your destination. It’s about enjoying the journey.” That phrase stuck with me. It made me realize that my mission statement couldn’t just be about survival or reaching goals. It had to be about thriving about living life fully, with purpose and joy.

With this new perspective, I began crafting my statement. To thrive, I needed passion—an excitement for what I did. I realized that without passion, it’s easy to burn out or feel unfulfilled, no matter how successful you are. But I also wanted my journey to include compassion. I had seen how much of a difference kindness could make, not just in my personal life but in the workplace. A little empathy goes a long way in building meaningful connections with others. Finally, I knew humour had to be a part of my mission. Life is hard enough as it is, and I’ve always believed that laughter makes the difficult moments a little more bearable.

Once I had refined my mission into what I now call my Platinum Statement, I began to feel its impact almost immediately. It became a sort of mental checkpoint that I returned to whenever I felt overwhelmed or lost. When deadlines were looming, or when I faced challenging decisions, I would remind myself: “Am I approaching this with passion, compassion, and humour?” It became my compass, guiding me through both the tough times and the good ones.

But the importance of this Platinum Statement wasn't just personal. Over time, I began to see why developing such a mission is valuable for anyone, in any stage of life or career. Here are a few reasons why I believe everyone should take the time to craft their own guiding statement:

Clarity and Purpose: A mission statement provides clarity. It helps you define what truly matters to you. Instead of being pulled in every direction by competing goals and demands, a mission statement centres your focus. You know what's important, and you're less likely to get distracted by things that don't align with your values.

Motivation and Focus: When you have a clear mission, it becomes easier to stay motivated. There are always going to be moments when you feel tired, discouraged, or uncertain. But a mission statement gives you a reason to keep pushing forward. It's your personal "why," and it helps you stay focused on what really matters.

Resilience: Life and work are full of ups and downs. A personal mission statement is a reminder of the bigger picture, especially during tough times. It helps you stay resilient by keeping you anchored to your purpose, even when the immediate challenges seem overwhelming.

Alignment: A well-crafted mission statement ensures that your actions are aligned with your values. It gives you a sense of integrity and purpose because your decisions and actions are in harmony with what you believe in. This alignment brings a deeper sense of satisfaction and fulfilment.

Inspiration for Others: When you live by your mission, you inspire those around you. Whether you realize it or not, people notice when you're passionate, compassionate, and able to laugh through life's challenges. You become a role model for others, showing them that it's possible to live and work with both purpose and joy.

As I started living by my Platinum Statement, I found that not only did it transform how I approached my work, but it also changed how I interacted with others. I became more intentional about fostering positive relationships with colleagues, clients, and even strangers. When things got stressful, instead of reacting with frustration, I reminded myself to approach the situation with compassion. And when something didn't go as planned, I tried to find humour in the situation rather than letting it ruin my day.

This mission statement also helped me discover new opportunities for growth. Because I was focused on thriving, not just surviving, I became more open to challenges that would help me grow, even if they were outside my comfort zone. I started volunteering for projects that excited me, even when I wasn't sure if I had all the answers. The passion in my Platinum Statement pushed me to take risks and embrace opportunities that I might have otherwise avoided.

Reflecting on this journey, I've realized that crafting a personal mission statement is more than just an exercise in self-reflection. It's a powerful tool that can shape your life in meaningful ways. For me, my Platinum Statement has become a daily reminder of who I am, what I stand for, and how I want to live. It's a reflection of my deepest values, and it inspires me to approach each day with energy, kindness, and a sense of humour.

So, I encourage everyone to take some time to craft their own statement. It doesn't have to be perfect at first—mine certainly wasn't. But as you reflect on your values, your goals, and the kind of life you want to lead, your statement will evolve, just as mine did. And once you have that guiding principle, you'll find that it becomes a powerful source of clarity, motivation, and fulfilment.

As I continue on my path, both in my career and personal life, my Platinum Statement remains my anchor. It reminds me that life is about more than just surviving the day-to-day grind—it's about thriving, about making each moment meaningful and joyful. And no matter what challenges come my way, I know I have a mission to guide me through, helping me live with passion, compassion, and a smile.

Punch Line : "Vision in Motion, Purpose in Sight, Crafting a Mission to Reach New Heights!"

Value 16 - The Art of Reading People

In my earlier years, I was obsessed with reading motivational books and autobiographies. Each time I picked one up, I was filled with excitement, hoping it would reveal the secrets of success. Every page was packed with wisdom, and I couldn't wait to apply what I learned to my own life. I devoured stories of successful individuals—entrepreneurs, athletes, leaders—believing that their experiences would guide me toward greatness. But despite all the knowledge I gathered, something was missing. I struggled to put those lessons into practice and saw little progress in my own life.

I vividly remember one particular autobiography that had me hooked. It was the story of a well-known entrepreneur who had overcome significant challenges to build a business empire. His determination and resilience were awe-inspiring, and I was convinced that if I followed his mindset, I'd see similar results. I tried to mimic his habits and adopt his way of thinking. But as time went on, I noticed something frustrating: while I was still motivated, I wasn't seeing the same kind of success. I was stuck in a loop of inspiration without real progress.

Weeks turned into months, and that initial burst of excitement started to fade. The words from the book that once felt powerful and motivating began to feel distant and disconnected from my own reality. The stories of triumph that had inspired me now felt like someone else's journey—something I couldn't quite relate to anymore.

Frustrated, I turned to other sources for inspiration. YouTube became my go-to place for motivational talks and interviews with successful people. I watched countless videos of speakers sharing their tips on success, growth, and achieving your dreams. I spent hours scrolling through social media, reading quotes from influencers who seemed to have life all figured out. It felt like I was always on the hunt for that one piece of advice that would spark a breakthrough and change everything for me.

But the more I consumed, the less clarity I had. Each piece of advice seemed disconnected from the next. One speaker would emphasize waking up at 5 a.m. every day to be successful, while another would swear by the importance of balance and rest. Some influencers talked about hustle and hard work, while others stressed mindfulness and self-care. It was as if I had collected a bunch of puzzle pieces that didn't fit together. Instead of feeling empowered, I felt overwhelmed and confused.

Then, one day, something shifted. I came across a simple quote that changed the way I thought about motivation: "Instead of reading motivational autobiographies, learn to read people." The words hit me like a revelation. I realized that while books and motivational talks could provide some value, they often felt too broad, too removed from the specific challenges I faced. The real lessons, I thought, might come from paying attention to the people around me—the ones who were living their lives with purpose and wisdom.

I decided to put this idea into practice. Instead of chasing after more books or videos, I started observing the people I interacted with every day. I focused on colleagues, friends, mentors—anyone who displayed qualities I admired. I paid attention to how they handled tough situations, how they communicated, and how they carried themselves through life's ups and downs.

One person, in particular, stood out—a senior executive at my company. He was the kind of leader who commanded respect without ever raising his voice. He had a calm confidence about him that made people listen when he spoke, and I admired the way he managed both successes and setbacks with grace. I began to closely observe him, not in a formal mentoring way but in the everyday moments—meetings, casual conversations, interactions with other team members.

I noticed how he navigated difficult meetings, always maintaining his composure even when things got heated. He had this ability to listen deeply before offering a solution, and his decisions were always thoughtful. He didn't just push people to work harder; he inspired them to want to work better. What struck me most was how he balanced authority with empathy. He never made anyone feel small, even when offering criticism, and his feedback always felt constructive rather than harsh.

As I watched him, I realized that success wasn't about following a single formula or copying someone's exact actions. It was about understanding the principles behind their behaviour and figuring out how to apply those principles in my own life. I didn't need to become a carbon copy of him; I needed to take what I admired and make it my own.

One day, I asked him how he managed to stay so calm under pressure. He smiled and said, "I've learned that reacting emotionally doesn't help anyone. I try to focus on the solution rather than the problem. People don't need someone to panic—they need someone to lead." His words stuck with me, and I began applying that mindset in my own work. When challenges arose, instead of reacting out of frustration or stress, I reminded myself to stay calm and focus on finding a way forward. It wasn't always easy, but the more I practiced, the more natural it felt.

This shift in my approach to learning and self-improvement was transformative. I realized that "reading" people—observing their actions, understanding their motivations, and learning from their experiences—was far more powerful than any book I had ever read. It wasn't about imitation; it was about assimilation. It was about taking the essence of what made someone successful and adapting it to fit my own circumstances.

For example, I learned that leadership wasn't just about giving orders or making decisions. It was about creating an environment where people felt valued and motivated. I saw how my mentor used empathy to build strong relationships with his team, and I started doing the same. I made an effort to listen more, to understand the challenges my colleagues were facing, and to offer support where I could. The result was a noticeable improvement in my relationships at workpeople responded more positively, and teamwork flourished.

I also learned that success wasn't about perfection. Watching my mentor, I saw that even the most successful people make mistakes. What mattered was how they responded to those mistakes. Instead of dwelling on failures, he would acknowledge them, learn from them, and move on with renewed focus. This approach helped me develop resilience. I stopped being so hard on myself when things didn't go as planned and started seeing setbacks as opportunities for growth.

Through this process, I came to understand that the most valuable lessons aren't always found in motivational books or inspirational talks. They're found in the people around us—the ones who live their values every day, who face challenges with courage and grace, and who show us that success is a personal journey, not a one-size-fits-all solution.

In the end, I learned that while books and speeches can offer inspiration, the real wisdom comes from life itself. By observing the people around, us, we gain insights that are practical, grounded, and applicable to our own lives. It's not about finding a magic formula for success—it's about understanding that the path to greatness is unique for each of us, and the best way to navigate it is by learning from the people who walk beside us.

So, whenever you feel stuck or in need of inspiration, look around. The people in your life may hold the key to unlocking your potential in ways no book ever could.

Punch Line: "Success isn't just a distant goal, it's learning from those who play the role!"

Value 17 - Realization at the Saloon Shop

It was an ordinary day, one that began just like any other. I followed my usual routine, completing my morning tasks and deciding it was time for my monthly haircut. I never missed these appointments—not just because I liked to stay well-groomed, but because it had become a ritual of sorts. The barber shop was only a short walk from my house, and after ten years of visiting the same place, it had evolved into more than just a spot for a trim. It was a place for conversation, a hub for local gossip, debates, and the occasional unsolicited life advice.

As I walked through the door, the familiar chime sounded, and my barber—who I had known for years—waved me over to the chair. He was a man with a knack for talking. In fact, he could probably strike up a lively conversation with a rock. Some days, I was prepared for the lengthy chats that accompanied my haircut. Other days, like today, I just wanted a quick trim without much fanfare. Little did I know, this would be one of those days where I wasn't quite prepared for what was to unfold.

I sat down in the chair, the familiar sound of scissors snipping filling the air. The barber, true to form, jumped right into a conversation. Today's topic? Cricket. Specifically, India's loss to Australia in a crucial match the night before.

"Can you believe it?" he began, his scissors flashing in the light. "Virat Kohli—he's completely forgotten how to play cricket! Did you see that ridiculous shot he played when five wickets were already down? Going for a six on a full toss ball? What a mistake! These international players, I tell you, they practice for hours and get paid crores only to get out for a few runs. Absolute nonsense!"

I nodded along, unable to respond verbally since he was now working on my beard, and I had to keep my face still. But the barber was in his element, and he certainly didn't need my input to keep the conversation going.

He moved from cricket to politics without missing a beat. "And don't even get me started on our Prime Minister, Shri Narendra Modi," he continued. "How can he justify all these foreign trips? The country is dealing with floods, unemployment, and corruption, and he's flying abroad like it's nothing! We have a Foreign Minister—Shri S. Jaishankar—let him manage those trips! Modi needs to stay here and focus on what really matters."

I listened, or at least half-listened, as he continued to voice his opinions with the conviction of someone who believed he knew exactly how to fix everything. Forty minutes passed with the barber passionately critiquing cricket strategies and political policies, and by the time he finally declared the haircut complete, I was relieved. Or so I thought.

As he dusted off the stray hairs from my neck and handed me a mirror to inspect his work, I was greeted with a rather unpleasant surprise. My hair was cut far shorter than usual, and one sideburn was significantly longer than the other. It was clear that in his excitement to discuss Virat Kohli's cricketing errors and Modi's foreign policy, the barber had neglected to pay attention to his own work.

I stared at the uneven haircut in the mirror for a moment, a mix of frustration and amusement building inside me. I looked up at him, still engrossed in his monologue about politics, seemingly unaware of the mess he had made.

“Mr. Barber,” I said, catching his attention, “you’ve spent the last 40 minutes telling me how Virat Kohli should play cricket and how the Prime Minister should handle his job. But in the meantime, you’ve forgotten to do your own job properly cutting hair!”

His eyes widened as the realization hit him. He stepped back, taking in the uneven sideburns and the patchy, too-short haircut. The irony of the situation wasn’t lost on him either. The barber, who had spent so much time criticizing others, had completely failed at the one task he was responsible for.

It was a small, everyday incident, but the lesson it left me with was far more significant. How often do we find ourselves criticizing or offering unsolicited advice on how others should do their jobs, all while neglecting our own responsibilities? It’s easy to point fingers, but much harder to focus on doing our own work well.

That experience stuck with me. We live in a world where everyone has an opinion about everything—how athletes should perform, how politicians should govern, how celebrities should behave. We spend so much time analysing and criticizing, often without taking a moment to reflect on our own performance. The truth is, it’s much easier to talk about what others should do than it is to do our own work with focus and care.

As I left the barber shop that day, I couldn’t help but chuckle at the situation. The barber had become so wrapped up in discussing what everyone else should be doing that he completely missed the fact that his own work was slipping. And the more I thought about it, the more I realized how common this behaviour is—not just in barber shops but in every part of life.

We often get distracted by conversations about things that don’t directly concern us, and in the process, we lose sight of what we're supposed to be doing. We offer advice, opinions, and critiques without truly understanding the complexities of someone else's job or life. Meanwhile, our own responsibilities—whether it's our career, our relationships, or our personal growth—are neglected.

This experience taught me an important lesson: Focus on doing your own work well before you start criticizing others. It's easy to offer advice from the sidelines, but it's much harder to excel in your own role. Whether you're a barber cutting hair, a professional managing a project, or simply someone trying to navigate life, the principle is the same—focus on your responsibilities and strive for excellence in whatever you do.

It also reminded me of the importance of self-awareness. How often do we really stop and assess our own performance? How often do we reflect on whether we're doing the best we can in our own roles? It's easy to get caught up in distractions, in irrelevant conversations, and in the endless stream of opinions that surround us. But true growth comes from focusing on what we can control—our own actions, our own work, and our own progress.

As I walked home with my uneven haircut that day, I realized that while it may not have been the best trim I'd ever received, the experience had given me something far more valuable—a reminder to always focus on doing my best, to avoid distractions, and to never let the noise of others drown out the importance of my own responsibilities.

And in the end, that lesson was worth more than the perfect haircut.

Key Takeaways:

Focus on Your Responsibilities: It's easy to criticize others, but it's more important to focus on doing your own work with excellence.

Avoid Distractions: Engaging in irrelevant conversations or opinions can distract you from the task at hand, leading to mistakes.

Self-Reflection: Before offering advice to others, reflect on whether you're effectively managing your own duties.

Quality of Work Matters: Your opinions won't matter if the quality of your own work isn't up to par.

Stay Humble: It's easy to spot flaws in others, but true growth comes from recognizing and improving your own shortcomings.

Punch Line: "Before you critique, take a closer peek—your own work may be the fix you seek!"

Value 18 - The Pareto Principle in Action

It was a late evening, one of those days when everything seemed to pile up at once. My desk was cluttered with tasks, each one demanding immediate attention, or at least that's how it seemed. Bills to pay, emails to respond to, a work presentation to prepare, and on top of all that, I had promised to take my family out for dinner. The overwhelming pressure pressed down on me like a weight, and I felt as if I were drowning in a sea of things to do.

As I sat there, staring at the chaos in front of me, a thought suddenly struck me—something I had read years ago but never really applied: the Pareto Principle, also known as the 80/20 rule. The idea behind it was simple yet powerful: 80% of the results come from 20% of the efforts. But how could this principle help me manage my life better? Was this the key to escaping the constant cycle of stress and pressure?

I decided to give it a try. With a deep breath, I grabbed a notepad and started jotting down everything I needed to do. The list seemed endless. Tasks seemed to multiply as soon as I wrote them down, each competing for my attention, each one screaming its own urgency. My mind buzzed with tension, but then I paused and asked myself an important question: "Which of these tasks will have the biggest impact on my life, either immediately or in the long term?"

This was the moment when everything changed for me.

As I glanced at the list, the answer wasn't immediately clear. All the tasks seemed to blur together in their urgency. But I took a step back and started really thinking about it—really thinking about it. I reflected on what would make the biggest difference, both for my peace of mind and my progress. Suddenly, I realized something: not all tasks were created equal. Sure, they all seemed urgent, but in reality, were they all important?

I circled a few tasks that stood out—those that, if completed, would make the biggest difference: finalizing the work presentation, paying the bills, and most importantly, spending quality time with my family. These were the tasks that mattered. These were my 20% tasks—the ones that would give me 80% of the satisfaction and progress I needed.

With newfound clarity, I got to work. First, I tackled the presentation, knowing that it was a critical part of my career and that completing it would relieve a lot of stress. I worked on it with laser focus, ignoring the emails, the clutter, the other distractions. I finished it quicker than I expected—once I gave it my undivided attention, it wasn't nearly as difficult as I had imagined.

Next, I quickly paid the bills, a task that had been hanging over my head for days. It took only a few minutes, but in those few minutes, I had lifted a huge weight off my shoulders. Financial worries had a way of nagging at me from the back of my mind, but now they were gone.

Finally, I shut down my laptop, put away the notepad, and focused entirely on my family. We went out for dinner as planned, and for the first time in weeks, I wasn't distracted by the mental clutter of unfinished tasks. I wasn't thinking about the work I had left to do or the emails that still needed answering. I was present—really present—with my family. We laughed, we talked, and we simply enjoyed each other's company. It was a simple dinner, but it felt special because I was there, not just physically but mentally and emotionally.

As we enjoyed our meal, I couldn't help but think about how much lighter I felt. By focusing on what truly mattered, I had freed myself from the pressure of trying to do everything at once. The tasks that I had initially thought were urgent—like replying to emails or tidying up my desk—could wait. They weren't going to make or break my day. For once, I realized that it was okay not to finish everything. It was okay to let some things wait if they weren't truly important.

The next morning, I woke up with a clear mind. I knew what needed to be done and in what order. The Pareto Principle had become more than just a concept; it was now a guiding force in my life. Whether it was managing my time at work, deciding how to spend my weekends, or even making decisions about long-term goals, I started applying the 80/20 rule consistently.

One area where this rule really started to make a difference was in my health. Like most people, I had tried to adopt countless new habits—new workout routines, new diets, new wellness trends—but I could never stick with them for long. I always felt like I was trying to do too much, and eventually, I would give up. But then I realized something: 80% of my well-being came from just 20% of my habits. The basics—regular exercise, a balanced diet, and sufficient sleep—were the foundation. Instead of chasing every new fitness trend or trying to overhaul my lifestyle all at once, I focused on these core habits. The results were incredible. I felt healthier, more energized, and less stressed about trying to "do it all."

Similarly, in my relationships, I began to apply the same thinking. I had many acquaintances, people I would occasionally see or chat with, but I realized that 80% of the joy and fulfilment in my relationships came from just a small handful of people.

These were the people who truly mattered—my closest friends and family. I made it a point to spend more time nurturing these relationships, rather than spreading myself thin across dozens of acquaintances. This shift not only deepened my connections with the people I loved but also made me feel more grounded, more fulfilled.

As these changes took root in my life, I began to see the bigger picture. The 80/20 rule wasn't just about managing tasks; it was about managing life. By focusing on the few things that truly mattered, I could achieve far more than by trying to do everything at once. It taught me to work smarter, not harder, and to live with intention rather than reaction. I learned to let go of the need to be constantly busy, and instead, I focused on being effective.

As I reflect on this journey, I realize that the Pareto Principle is more than just a productivity hack—it's a philosophy for living a balanced, meaningful life. It's about recognizing that you can't do everything, but if you focus on the right things, you'll achieve far more than you ever thought possible.

So, the next time you feel overwhelmed, take a step back and ask yourself: What's the 20% that will make the biggest difference? Prioritize those tasks, and you'll find that the rest often takes care of itself.

Punch Line: "Focus on the few, let the rest fall through—less is more, and it'll all come true!"

Value 19 - How Negative Thinking Helped Me Succeed

In a world full of motivational talks and books urging us to think positively, my approach might sound a bit strange. While everyone says you should always stay optimistic, I've often found that thinking about what could go wrong has actually worked out well for me.

I know it might seem odd. How can focusing on potential failures and setbacks possibly help? But time and again, I've discovered that this way of thinking has been a key part of my success.

Let me share a story from a few years ago.

I was working on a major project that was very important for my career. The pressure was intense, and everyone around me was super positive. They kept telling me, "Don't worry, you'll do great. Just focus on success." Their words were meant to encourage me, but I couldn't shake off the nagging thoughts that filled my mind. I kept thinking about all the things that could go wrong. What if the project failed? What if I missed something crucial?

Instead of pushing these thoughts away, I did something that many would consider counterproductive: I allowed myself to think them through. I wasn't trying to be negative, but rather, I was being realistic. There was a strange sense of calm that came from acknowledging potential pitfalls rather than ignoring them. Instead of running from these doubts, I started to analyse them.

This mindset didn't make me anxious—it actually motivated me. The fear of failure made me more careful and detailed in my work. I started looking at every part of the project, searching for potential problems and figuring out how to manage them before they even happened. It felt like I was playing chess, constantly thinking several steps ahead. Not just about winning, but about what obstacles might arise and how I could counter them.

As the project moved forward, I continued to prepare for anything that might go wrong. When issues did arise, I was ready for them. My so-called "negative" thinking wasn't holding me back; it was pushing me forward, making sure I was prepared and focused. Small setbacks didn't throw me off course because I had already anticipated them and had a plan in place.

When the project turned out to be a big success, I couldn't help but reflect on the journey. Would things have gone as smoothly if I had only focused on positive thoughts? Would I have been as thorough? Would I have caught potential problems early on? I'm not sure, but I do know that my cautious approach played a big role in making sure everything went according to plan.

This wasn't a one-time thing. Over the years, I've found that negative thinking—when used in the right way—can be really powerful. It's not about being a pessimist or expecting failure. It's about being prepared for anything and using that preparation to your advantage. By thinking about what could go wrong, I'm able to make sure things go right.

Another example comes from a personal experience that had nothing to do with business but everything to do with caution.

A couple of years ago, I was planning a long trek with some friends to a remote area known for its beauty but also for its unpredictability. The weather in that region could change in an instant, and the trails were known to be challenging. While my friends were excited and ready to go, my mind immediately started thinking about all the potential dangers. What if the weather turned bad? What if someone got injured? What if we got lost?

I couldn't ignore these thoughts, so I decided to prepare for them. I researched the area thoroughly, learning everything I could about the terrain and weather patterns. I packed extra supplies, made sure we had proper maps, and even went as far as learning some basic first aid, just in case.

When we finally set out on the trek, it started off beautifully. The weather was perfect, and the scenery was breathtaking. We were all in high spirits, but halfway through, just as I had feared, the weather took a sudden turn for the worse. Dark clouds rolled in, and within minutes, a storm descended upon us. The trails became slippery and dangerous, and visibility dropped too almost nothing.

But because I had anticipated this possibility and prepared for it, we were able to find shelter quickly and stay safe. My friends, who had been so confident at the beginning, later admitted that they hadn't thought about what could go wrong, and they were grateful that I had. My so-called "negative" thinking had saved the day.

This experience reinforced for me the value of negative thinking. It's not about expecting the worst, but about being prepared for it. It's about balancing confidence with caution, making sure you're ready for whatever challenges might come your way.

Negative thinking has also kept me from becoming overconfident. It's easy to get carried away by success and start believing nothing can go wrong. But that's when mistakes happen—when you stop being careful and stop preparing for the unexpected. By allowing myself to think negatively, I've stayed grounded and avoided those pitfalls. I've learned to walk a fine line between optimism and realism, and it's made all the difference.

Over time, I've come to realize that negative thinking, in moderation, can be just as important as positive thinking. The key is how you use it. For me, it's never been about dwelling on failures or expecting the worst. Instead, it's about acknowledging that challenges are inevitable and that being prepared for them is the smartest thing you can do.

In the end, I've learned that while positive thinking is important, it's not the only way to approach life. Negative thinking, when done thoughtfully, can be just as helpful. It keeps you sharp, focused, and ready for whatever comes your way. It's a tool—one that's often overlooked but has the potential to make a huge difference in how we navigate life's challenges.

As I sit back and reflect on my journey, I can say with confidence that negative thinking has played a crucial role in my success. It's helped me stay prepared, avoid unnecessary risks, and make more thoughtful decisions. It might not be the most popular mindset, but for me, it's been incredibly effective.

So, the next time you face a big decision or a difficult challenge, don't be afraid to think about what could go wrong. Embrace those thoughts, prepare for them, and use them to your advantage. You might just find that negative thinking can lead to some very positive outcomes.

Punch Line : "Turn Doubts into Drive, Let Negative Thoughts Help You Thrive!"

Value 20 - Late Realization of Self-Discipline

Discipline is something we hear about all the time—whether it's in school, at work, or during motivational talks. It's one of those words that gets tossed around so often that it can start to lose its meaning. At least, that's how it was for me. For years, I heard people talking about the importance of discipline, but I never really understood what it meant in a way that resonated with me. I certainly didn't realize how crucial it was until much later in life.

It wasn't a life-changing event or some grand realization that brought the importance of discipline to light for me. It happened during a simple, almost routine moment—one of those times where you wouldn't expect to learn anything profound. It was during my 30s, well into my career and personal routine, while I was working out. I had been exercising regularly for a while, not for any special reason, just as part of my everyday schedule. But that one day, during a regular session of push-ups, something unexpected happened.

I was halfway through my usual reps when I suddenly felt off. I wasn't in the mood to push myself. Maybe I was tired, or maybe I just didn't feel motivated that day. Whatever the reason, I decided to cut my reps short. I figured, "What's the harm in skipping a few push-ups? It's not like anyone else is watching or counting." I stood up, ready to brush it off and move on with my day.

But as I got up, I paused. A strange thought hit me. Who was I cheating by skipping those push-ups? Was there anyone I had to answer to? No one was standing over me, keeping track of what

I did. It was just me. And in that moment, it clicked: I was cheating myself.

It might sound small, even trivial, but that realization had a profound impact on me. The idea that I was the only one who really knew whether or not I followed through on my commitment stayed with me. I couldn't shake it. Sure, no one else would ever know if I cut a few corners, but I knew. I was the one keeping track. And I would be the one who had to live with that knowledge.

For days, this thought echoed in my mind. How often do we cheat ourselves without even realizing it? How often do we slack off on our goals, skip parts of our routines, or tell ourselves that missing a step here or there won't matter? We think, "It's no big deal." But the truth is, we can't escape our own accountability. Our inner selves—the part of us that knows when we're cutting corners—always keep score, even if no one else notices.

That simple moment of skipping a few push-ups turned into something much bigger for me. I started thinking about all the other areas of my life where I had been less than disciplined. Whether it was in my work, my personal goals, or even in my relationships, I realized that discipline wasn't just about following a set of rules or sticking to a schedule. It was about being true to myself.

For so long, I had viewed discipline as something external. I thought it was about meeting expectations set by others—whether it was at work, in fitness, or in life in general. But I began to see it differently. Discipline, at its core, is deeply personal. It's not about doing things because someone else expects you to; it's about holding yourself accountable to your own standards. It's about following through on your commitments to yourself, even when no one else is watching.

That realization sparked a shift in how I approached everything. I began to focus less on doing things because I "had to" and more on doing them because I wanted to hold myself to a higher standard. I started seeing discipline as a form of self-respect, a way of showing myself that my goals and commitments mattered. Whether it was in my workouts, my career, or even my daily habits, I stopped making excuses. I stopped allowing myself to cut corners just because it was easier.

At first, it wasn't easy. There were plenty of times when I was tempted to fall back into old habits. There were days when I didn't feel like going the extra mile, when taking shortcuts felt like the natural thing to do. But every time I felt tempted to give in, I reminded myself of that moment during my workout—the moment I realized that I was only cheating myself. And with that reminder, I pushed through.

What I found was that the more I committed to being disciplined, the better I felt about everything in my life. There was a sense of satisfaction that came from knowing I was giving my best, even when no one else was watching. It wasn't about being perfect or never making mistakes—it was about doing what I knew was right, for me.

Looking back, I wish I had learned this lesson earlier. I spent so many years going through the motions, thinking that as long as I met the basic requirements, I was doing enough. But I see now that true discipline isn't about doing the bare minimum. It's about challenging yourself to do more, to be better, not because someone else expects it, but because you expect it from yourself.

This new understanding of discipline didn't just improve my workouts or my productivity at work—it changed how I viewed everything. It made me more mindful of how I spent my time, how I approached my goals, and even how I interacted with the people around me. I started to take ownership of my life in a way I hadn't before. Instead of drifting through my days, I became more intentional. I started to value my time and my efforts more.

In the end, discipline became a cornerstone of my life, but not in the way I had originally thought. It wasn't about following strict rules or sticking to a rigid routine. It was about being honest with myself. It was about holding myself accountable, even when it would have been easier to let things slide. It was about showing myself that I was worth the effort.

And perhaps the most surprising thing I learned is that discipline, when done right, isn't a burden. It's a gift. It's a way of making sure that you're living your life in alignment with your values and goals. It's a way of respecting yourself and your potential. When you approach discipline this way, it stops feeling like a chore and starts feeling like a powerful tool for growth.

So now, whenever I feel tempted to take the easy way out, I remind myself of that simple workout session—the one where I almost cheated myself out of a few push-ups. It's a small reminder, but it carries a big message: you are your own accountability. No one else can hold you to the standards you set for yourself. Only you can do that. And once you start embracing discipline not as something you "have to do" but as something you deserve, everything else starts to fall into place.

In the end, discipline isn't just about following rules; it's about living with integrity, staying true to your goals, and never settling for less than your best.

Punch Line: "Stay true to your plan, and you'll rise like no one can!"

Value 21 - The Illusion of Success Stories

There was a time when I was completely captivated by motivational talks. You know, the kind that YouTube and social media constantly throw at you—those videos where highly successful people share their journeys, filled with struggles, hard work, countless rejections, moments of failure, and eventually, their triumphant comeback that led them to where they are now. It seemed like every successful person had a story worth hearing, and I was eager to absorb every word, hoping that their experiences would somehow inspire me to greatness.

I remember countless late nights spent in the quiet of my room, eyes glued to the screen, hanging on every word these achievers said. They spoke with passion about discovering their true potential, pushing through their darkest days, and how everything eventually fell into place for them. Their stories were so powerful, so moving, that it was easy to get lost in them. I found myself imagining walking a similar path, facing challenges with unwavering resolve, and eventually emerging victorious, just like them.

But one day, something dawned on me—something so simple yet so profound that it completely shifted my perspective. As I sat there, mesmerized by another success story, I realized that while these stories were incredibly inspiring, they were all told in hindsight. These people were sharing their journeys from the vantage point of success, looking back with clarity and insight that only comes after you've reached the finish line. They could easily connect the dots, highlight the pivotal moments, and create a narrative that made it all seem like part of a grand plan.

But then I wondered, what about the actual moments they were in? What were they really feeling when they were going through those struggles, rejections, and failures? Were they aware that these hardships would one day make for a great story? Did they have any idea that they were on a path to greatness? I highly doubted it. This thought led me to reflect on my own life—now at 40—and I realized that I, too, could recount my successes and failures in a way that could be both inspiring and entertaining. I could craft a story that would make others believe that I was some kind of resilient hero who always knew how to manage life's challenges.

Yet, if I were to go back to those exact moments when I was in the thick of it, I would find that I wasn't thinking about any grand lessons or future success. I was just living, dealing with each situation as it came, doing what I thought was best at the time. There was no script, no grand plan unfolding in my mind. It was just life happening, and I was along for the ride, trying to navigate through the ups and downs as best as I could.

This realization hit me hard. It made me see that success stories, as inspiring as they are, can be an illusion. They are a way of making sense of the past with the benefit of hindsight. After achieving something, it's easy to look back and talk about the process as if it were all part of a well-thought-out plan. But when you're in the middle of that process, it's a completely different story. There's uncertainty, fear, doubt, and a lot of improvisation. You don't always know what you're doing or where you're headed. You just keep moving forward, hoping that things will work out in the end. So, I decided to stop obsessing over other people's success stories. I realized that while it's nice to be inspired by them, they aren't a roadmap for my own life. Instead of getting lost in someone else's journey, I started focusing more on my own. I began to experience my path towards success as it came, moment by moment, doing the best I could with what I had. I learned to embrace the uncertainty, the mistakes, and the unexpected twists and turns, knowing that each experience was either bringing me closer to my goals or teaching me something valuable.

This shift in perspective was liberating. It allowed me to live more authentically, without the pressure of measuring up to someone else's story. I stopped comparing my journey to others and started appreciating it for what it was—my own unique experience. I realized that success is not about following someone else's script; it's about writing your own, even if you don't always know how the story will end.

And that's what this book is about living the journey, not just for the sake of creating a good story to tell later, but for the sake of living fully in the present. It's about doing your best, accepting the outcomes, and continuing to grow, no matter what. Because in the end, success isn't about the story you tell; it's about the life you live.

One of the biggest problems with success stories is that they often gloss over the messiness of the process. They don't always show the sleepless nights, the anxiety, the moments of self-doubt, or the times when you just want to give up. They don't talk about the times when you have no idea if what you're doing will lead to anything at all. Instead, they focus on the highlights—the moments of triumph, the breakthroughs, the happy endings.

But life isn't just a series of highlights. It's a mix of good days and bad days, of successes and failures, of steps forward and steps backward. And that's okay. It's all part of the process. What matters is not how perfectly you follow someone else's path, but how you navigate your own. It's about being honest with yourself, embracing your journey with all its imperfections, and finding meaning in the moments that don't always make it into the success stories.

For me, this meant letting go of the idea that I needed to have everything figured out. It meant accepting that it's okay to feel lost sometimes, to not have all the answers, and to make mistakes along the way. It meant trusting that even when things don't go according to plan, there's still value in the experience. Every setback, every failure, every detour is a part of the journey. They don't define your success, but they do shape who you become.

So, I started living with more intention, not worrying so much about the end result but focusing on the process. I began to appreciate the small wins, the lessons learned, and the personal growth that comes from just showing up every day and doing the work. I stopped looking for shortcuts and started trusting in the journey, knowing that the story I'm writing isn't just about the successes, but also about the resilience, the perseverance, and the willingness to keep going, no matter what.

In the end, I realized that the true measure of success isn't how your story sounds to others, but how it feels to you. It's about living a life that's true to yourself, one where you can look back and say, "I did my best with what I had, and I lived fully." That's the kind of success that doesn't need to be turned into a story, because it's not about impressing others. It's about finding peace and fulfilment in your own journey, knowing that you've made the most of the life you've been given.

So, if you find yourself getting caught up in other people's success stories, take a step back. Remember that those stories are just that—stories. They are polished versions of someone's journey, told with the clarity of hindsight. But your journey is happening right now, in real-time, with all its messiness and uncertainty. Embrace it. Live it. And trust that, in the end, the life you live will be the greatest story you ever tell.

Punch Line : "Success isn't about the story you tell—it's about the life you live."

Value 22 - Mastering the Art of Self-Learning

Very early in my life, I stumbled upon one of the most valuable realizations that would shape my journey: the power of self-learning. I can't pinpoint exactly when or how it happened, but I came to understand that what I studied in school and college would not be enough to build the career I envisioned. Perhaps it was a series of small incidents, moments where I found myself lacking the knowledge or skills needed to navigate the challenges ahead. Whatever the trigger, it became clear that if I wanted to succeed, I would have to take my education into my own hands.

It wasn't a grand revelation, but rather a quiet understanding that gradually took root. I had always been a good student, but something about the traditional education system felt incomplete. I realized that while school taught me the basics, it wasn't equipping me with the skills I needed for the real world. The deeper knowledge I craved wasn't going to come from a textbook or a classroom—it would have to come from me.

So, I began a journey of self-learning.

It started in the simplest way—by identifying the gaps in my knowledge. I made a mental list of the things I knew I needed to improve or explore further: financial management, stock investment, artificial intelligence, startup investing, and even LinkedIn mastery—these were just a few of the topics on my list. It was a bit overwhelming at first, realizing how much I didn't know, but I was determined to close those gaps.

The first step in this journey was finding the right sources of information. In a world where knowledge is abundant, the real challenge is filtering through the noise to find what's truly valuable. I began by following specific channels that focused on the topics I wanted to learn. Whether it was YouTube, blogs, or online forums, I became meticulous about the content I consumed. I made it a point to limit distractions and focused on materials that aligned with my goals. The beauty of social media is that it adapts to your interests—the more I engaged with content on financial management or artificial intelligence, the more my feeds were filled with useful resources.

At this point, I wasn't spending any money on my learning—everything was freely available if I knew where to look. The internet became my classroom, and I was both the student and the teacher. Self-discipline was key. There was no one to tell me what to learn or when to do it; I had to create that structure for myself.

Then, I discovered another powerful tool: free webinars. These were gold mines of information. Since I had narrowed down my interests, I started seeing ads for webinars that matched my needs. It was fascinating how social media worked—it knew what I was interested in and served me more of it. These free webinars were incredibly useful. Sure, at the end of each session, there was always a pitch for paid services, but even the free content was packed with valuable information. I didn't feel pressured to buy anything. I simply took what I could, learned from it, and implemented those insights.

But as with any journey, I soon hit a point where the free resources weren't enough. I realized that to get more advanced knowledge, I would need to invest a bit. That's when I started attending paid webinars, which ranged from ₹99 to ₹199. It wasn't a huge financial commitment, but the return was immense. These sessions were far more in-depth, offering insights and strategies that I hadn't come across in the free versions. The speakers were often industry experts, and they provided actionable advice that I could implement immediately.

Slowly but surely, I could feel myself levelling up. I was no longer just collecting knowledge—I was applying it, evaluating it in real-world scenarios, and seeing the results. Whether it was learning how to manage my finances better or understanding the basics of artificial intelligence, I could feel the tangible benefits of my efforts. It wasn't just about learning for the sake of learning anymore; it was about gaining skills that would make me more effective and confident in my decisions.

One of the most interesting parts of this journey was the age of the influencers and teachers I followed. Many of them were younger than me, sometimes significantly so. At first, it struck me as surprising. Here I was, learning about advanced financial strategies or tech innovations from people who were in their twenties. It made me wonder—how did they know so much at such a young age? What had taken me years to figure out seemed to come naturally to them.

But instead of feeling discouraged, I found it inspiring. These young teachers had embraced the power of self-learning early on. They hadn't waited for formal education to give them the tools they needed; they had gone out and found it themselves. In doing so, they had leapfrogged ahead, mastering skills that most people didn't acquire until much later in life. This was a powerful lesson for me—it showed me that age or experience wasn't the defining factor in success. What mattered was initiative and the willingness to learn on your own terms.

This realization also taught me something else: the need to keep my ego in check. It's easy to feel uncomfortable when you're learning from someone younger or less experienced in life. Your pride can get in the way, making you think, "I should already know this" or "I shouldn't be taking advice from someone half my age." But self-learning requires humility. The moment you think you know it all is the moment you stop growing.

As I continued on my self-learning journey, I learned to let go of that ego. Whether the information came from a seasoned professional or a young influencer, I stayed open-minded. I reminded myself that every bit of knowledge was valuable, no matter where it came from. What mattered was that I was moving forward, expanding my horizons, and becoming better in the process.

Ultimately, what I discovered is that self-learning is about more than just acquiring knowledge. It's about taking control of your growth, being proactive in your education, and constantly pushing yourself to improve. In today's world, traditional education is just the beginning. The real journey begins when you take matters into your own hands and start learning on your own terms.

Looking back, I can see that this decision to embrace self-learning was one of the most important I've ever made. It gave me the flexibility to learn what I wanted, at my own pace, and on my own terms. It allowed me to adapt to the changing demands of the world, constantly evolving and staying relevant. Most importantly, it showed me that I didn't need to wait for permission to grow—I could do it myself.

In the end, self-learning is a journey that never really ends. There's always more to learn, more to explore, more to understand. But that's the beauty of it. It's not about reaching a final destination; it's about the continuous process of becoming better every day. And for me, that's what makes it so rewarding. Punch line: "To grow and thrive, let self-learning drive."

Value 23 – Realizing the True Value of Parents Over Professional Bosses

In the early days of my career, I was fortunate enough to start working for one of the biggest and most reputed automobile manufacturers in India. The company was renowned for its work culture and ethics, values that became deeply ingrained in me from the moment I stepped out of college and into the professional world. Over the years, as I transitioned through various companies, this culture of respect, particularly towards the boss, was something I carried with me. I had been conditioned to believe that the boss was almost like a king—a figure of authority to be respected, and sometimes even feared, as though he was personally responsible for signing my pay check.

The word "BOSS" itself seemed to carry a weight of dominance and power. And I, like many others, was no exception to this norm. Even at the age of 40, I found myself respecting my bosses without question. I never argued, always maintained a pleasant demeanour, and even if I didn't agree with something they said, I would keep it to myself. Instead, I would nod, accept it, try to implement their suggestions, and always respond with a "Yes, Sir!" or "Will do it, Sir!" Even if I was in the middle of something important, if a call came from my boss, I would drop everything, answer immediately, listen attentively, and respond with utmost politeness.

It wasn't just professional; it felt personal. Pleasing the boss had become almost second nature to me. After all, I had grown up in a culture where hierarchy was respected, and authority figures were treated with a certain reverence. For years, this pattern of behaviour followed me, and I never really questioned it.

But life has a strange way of teaching us lessons, often in moments of deep reflection, moments we least expect. It was only after my father passed away that I had one such moment—a moment that would shift my perspective entirely.

One afternoon, not long after my father's passing, I sat down to compile our family's assets and financial data. It was a mundane task, something that needed to be done. But as I started to go through the numbers, something struck me hard. My father had left behind a significant amount of money, a safety net that I had never fully appreciated before. Out of pure curiosity, I began comparing my annual salary to the value of the assets my father had quietly accumulated over the years. The numbers were staggering. The savings, properties, and securities my father had built up were worth far more than I earned, or could hope to earn, in several years.

And then, a thought crept into my mind—something unsettling. For so many years, I had worked under various bosses, bending over backward to please them. I had spent an average of two to three years in each company, always with the same mindset: don't upset the boss, keep him happy, or else I might lose my job. Even at my first job, where I stayed for eight years, I operated with this mentality. In those years, I worked late, answered calls at all hours, and constantly worried about how my work would be perceived by my superiors.

But as I sat there with those figures in front of me, a harsh reality hit me. I had spent years of my life being cautious around my bosses, treating them with the utmost respect, while taking my parents for granted. I had always been careful not to upset my bosses, always ensuring I was on good terms with them. But when it came to my parents, I had often been casual, even argumentative. I had shown them my disappointments, my frustrations, without a second thought.

The irony was painfully clear. The assets my father had left for me—his years of hard work and sacrifice—were far more valuable than anything my bosses could ever offer. Yet, I had shown more care and respect to people who were in my life for a few years at most, rather than to my own parents, who had given me everything.

This realization hit me like a ton of bricks. All those times I had tried to please my bosses, all the energy I had spent worrying about their opinions, seemed so insignificant now. The real VIPs in my life, the ones who had given me everything without expecting anything in return, were my parents. And yet, I had been more focused on impressing people who, in the grand scheme of things, didn't really matter as much.

I sat there in deep reflection, a profound sense of regret settling over me. I wished I had understood sooner that the respect and care I had shown to my bosses should have been directed towards my parents first. They were the ones who had made countless sacrifices for me. They were the ones who had always been there, offering support, encouragement, and love, without ever asking for anything in return. And yet, I had treated them with less regard than I had treated my professional superiors.

It's strange how life's most valuable lessons often come to us too late. Sitting there, thinking about my father and the legacy he left behind, I couldn't help but feel a deep sadness. I wished I had taken the time to show my parents the same level of respect and attention that I had given to people who were just a small part of my life. I wished I had realized that the most important people in my life weren't those signing my pay check, but the ones who had given me everything long before I had even entered the workforce.

This experience taught me a critical lesson: the people who love us unconditionally—our parents, our family—deserve our utmost respect and care. It's easy to get caught up in the professional world, where we are constantly trying to impress and please others. But at the end of the day, the people who truly matter are the ones who have been there for us through thick and thin, who have supported us in ways we may never fully appreciate.

I carry this lesson with me now, every day. The people who mean the most to us should never be taken for granted. They are irreplaceable, and their value in our lives far exceeds any professional relationship we might have. It's a truth I now hold close to my heart, and one I wish I had understood much earlier in life.

In the end, respect and gratitude should be reserved for the ones who truly deserve it—those who have been with us from the very beginning, supporting us not because they have to, but because they love us. Our bosses may come and go, but our family, especially our parents, are the ones who stand by us through it all. And that's something I'll never forget again.

Punch Line : "Bosses come and go, but parents' love will always flow."

Value 24 - "Detours to Destiny: How I Found Success on the Road Less Travelled"

After completing my secondary education, I found myself at a crossroads, unsure of which path to follow. While most of my peers were heading toward pre-university courses and planning their journeys to prestigious colleges, I was dealing with family pressure to take a different route. My family wanted me to start working as soon as possible, so they pushed me to enrol in a diploma course in mechanical engineering—a three-year program designed to get me into the workforce more quickly.

The decision, at first glance, seemed practical. It would save me three years compared to the traditional route of pre-university followed by a bachelor's degree in engineering. I would be ahead of my peers in entering the job market. But deep inside, I felt a growing sense of regret. It felt as though I had taken a detour off the highway of life and onto a side road, missing out on the opportunities that come with a full-fledged degree and the sense of prestige that came with it.

A Quiet Regret

Despite my disappointment, I completed my diploma. Fortunately, and somewhat unexpectedly, I landed a job at one of the top automotive companies. It felt like a stroke of divine grace, but even as I began my career, the regret still lingered. I couldn't help but dwell on the fact that I hadn't pursued the traditional path, wondering if this decision would haunt me throughout my professional life. My peers were in university, living the student life, while I was already working—but I felt like I was missing out on something fundamental. Would my lack of a proper degree hold me back?

The first year of my job was shadowed by this internal struggle. I put on a brave face, but inside, I felt uncertain about my future. I kept asking myself if I had made the right choice, whether I had sacrificed long-term potential for short-term practicality. But as fate would have it, a new opportunity was about to present itself.

A New Door Opens

After a year, I was transferred to another city as part of my job. It was a move that initially felt routine, but it turned out to be a turning point in my life. By sheer luck—or perhaps fate—I discovered an evening college in that city offering a bachelor's degree in mechanical engineering. The only catch was that to enrol, I needed to have completed one year of work experience and pass an entrance exam.

The moment I heard about this, something clicked inside me. I knew this was my second chance. I decided that no matter the obstacles, I would take the entrance exam and secure a spot in the program. It felt like my way of getting back on the highway I had detoured from.

I threw myself into preparation for the exam with everything I had. It wasn't easy juggling a full-time job and preparing for the entrance test, but I was determined. And when the results came in, I couldn't believe it—I had secured the 2nd rank. I was in. It felt like a massive victory, a chance to make up for the path I hadn't taken earlier.

A New Challenge

However, getting into the program was only the beginning of my challenge. The real hurdle lay ahead: getting permission from my company to attend evening classes. The college ran its sessions from 6 pm to 10 pm, but my job required me to work the 2nd shift, which clashed with the class timings.

Since I was the first person in the company to make such a request, there was no precedent. Initially, my reporting manager wasn't very supportive, and it seemed like my dreams might end before they even began. But there was a glimmer of hope. The company agreed to allow me to attend college on one condition—I had to find a colleague who would be willing to cover my 2nd shift while I managed the 1st and night shifts.

At first, I thought it was an impossible condition. Who would be willing to take on extra work just to help me out? But as luck would have it, my colleague Rehman, along with a few others, stepped forward and volunteered to cover my 2nd shifts. I will forever be grateful to them for their kindness and support. Without their help, my dream of earning a degree might have remained just that—a dream.

A Gruelling Routine

The next three years of my life were nothing short of relentless. My days started at 4:30 in the morning when I'd wake up to catch the company bus at 5:20 am. I worked until 4:30 pm, then immediately rushed home, grabbed my bike, and rode 30 kilometres to college. Classes ran from 6 pm to 10 pm, and afterward, I'd attend a late-night tuition session from 10 to 11:30 pm to make up for anything I missed during regular class hours. The routine was exhausting, but I was determined. I only managed a few hours of sleep each night, and Sundays were no exception. In fact, Sundays were often the hardest. I would spend my entire day doing practical work from 7 am to 2 pm, followed by extra classes for subjects like mathematics and engineering drawing—subjects we had missed out on since we joined the course in the second year.

My weekly cycle didn't just involve long days; it included night shifts as well. Every Monday, I would head straight from college to work the night shift from 10 pm to 6 am. And Saturdays were the most gruelling of all. I had to work the entire night shift, finishing at 6 am Sunday morning, only to head straight to college for practical. There were times when I didn't sleep at all, running on pure determination and willpower.

This routine wasn't just challenging physically—it took a mental and emotional toll. But the one thing that kept me going was my goal. I knew why I was doing it, and I kept reminding myself that this was my chance to change my path. I had missed out on something earlier in life, but now I was working hard to reclaim it.

A Rewarding Finish

After three years of relentless effort, the day finally came when I completed my bachelor's degree in mechanical engineering. It felt like I had climbed a mountain. I had made it back onto the highway, overcoming every obstacle that had been placed in my way. The sense of accomplishment was immense, but more than that, there was a deep sense of relief. I had proven to myself that it was never too late to change my course, and that with hard work and determination, I could achieve what I once thought I had lost.

Looking back now, the whole experience feels almost unreal. At the time, I wasn't thinking about how difficult it was. My focus was always on the next step—getting through each day, balancing work, and studies, and moving closer to my goal. It wasn't about heroism or perseverance; it was about survival and progress. One day at a time.

What this chapter of my life taught me is that even if you take a detour, it's never too late to correct your course. There might be hardships, sacrifices, and obstacles in the way, but if you're determined, you can find your way back. In fact, sometimes the detour can give you unexpected advantages. In my case, I ended up with three years of professional experience while earning my degree, something my peers in traditional university programs didn't have.

The Lesson

The greatest lesson I learned from this experience is that life doesn't always go according to plan, and that's okay. It's not the path you take that defines you—it's how you navigate the challenges along the way. The road less travelled may seem more difficult at times, but it can also lead to unexpected rewards.

I hope my story inspires others who may feel trapped by their circumstances or overwhelmed by life's challenges. No matter what detours you face, no matter how far off course you feel, there's always a way to change your direction. With determination, support, and a clear sense of purpose, you can turn things around and achieve your dreams.

So, here's to the detours in life—the unexpected paths that shape who we become. They may be tough, but they make the journey that much more rewarding when we finally reach our destination.

Punch line: "From Side Road to Success, With Grit and Progress!"

Value 25 - The Turning Point— Realising True meaning of 'Net – Work; Net – Worth'

If someone were to ask me today what my most significant achievement in life is, I wouldn't tell them about the national awards I've won or the various professional accolades I've collected over the years. Those are all important, sure, but they pale in comparison to what I consider my greatest success. Without hesitation, I would proudly tell them about the strong professional network I've built on LinkedIn.

With over 65,000 valuable followers, 40% of whom are founders, CEOs, presidents, directors, and senior leaders, and an impressive 34 million impressions on my posts, this network stands as my proudest accomplishment. It's not just about the numbers, though; it's about the relationships and opportunities those numbers represent. This achievement is the result of years of commitment, consistency, and, above all, a deep trust in the power of LinkedIn as a platform for growth.

The Humble Beginning

My journey with LinkedIn began back in 2012. It's hard to believe now, but in those early days, I didn't quite understand what LinkedIn had to offer. I regret to admit that I wasted the first four years treating it like just another social media platform, not realizing that it was actually a goldmine for professional networking and growth. I used LinkedIn passively, connecting with a few colleagues here and there, posting sporadically, and not thinking much of it.

I treated it like a digital resume—something to keep updated but not interactive. Back then, LinkedIn didn't seem like the bustling hub of opportunity it is today. I was missing the bigger picture. I thought the connections were simply names on a list, not realizing the immense value that came from engaging with those names and building real relationships. I let opportunities slip through my fingers because I wasn't paying attention.

But as they say, better late than never. Around 2016, everything changed. I began to understand what LinkedIn could really be—a powerful tool to shape my professional future.

The Turning Point

The turning point came when I saw others using LinkedIn in ways I hadn't imagined. I noticed a few individuals who were regularly sharing thoughtful content, building large followings, and more importantly, opening doors for themselves through the platform. They weren't just posting about their jobs or companies; they were sharing insights, offering advice, and starting meaningful conversations. That's when it hit me—LinkedIn was not just a platform for job seekers or recruiters. It was a place for people to establish themselves as thought leaders, create value, and build connections that matter.

Realizing this, I have dived headfirst into learning and mastering LinkedIn. I had no guidebook, no mentor to show me the ropes. Instead, I learned through trial and error. I started by posting content that resonated with my expertise, sharing stories, and engaging with the posts of others. The more I participated, the more I learned. I began to experiment with different types of content—videos, articles, personal stories—and I watched closely to see what worked and what didn't. It was a long process, but it was worth every moment.

Building the Network

Slowly but surely, I began to build my network organically. At first, it felt like a grind. There were no shortcuts. I connected with people who shared my professional interests and who could offer insights that I wouldn't have access to otherwise. I reached out to leaders in my industry, engaging with their content, and making myself known not as someone looking for Favors, but as someone who wanted to learn and grow.

One of the biggest mistakes people make on LinkedIn is treating it like a numbers game. It's not about how many connections you have; it's about the quality of those connections. I didn't want to just add people to my network for the sake of it. I wanted to build meaningful relationships with professionals who could add value to my journey and whose journeys I could contribute to as well. That's how real networking happens—not through cold connection requests but through genuine engagement and shared interests.

Daily Motivation

Today, when I wake up in the morning, my first motivation comes from scrolling through my LinkedIn connection requests. There's something incredibly satisfying about seeing messages from CEOs, founders, directors, and senior leaders who want to connect with me—people who value what I bring to the table. It's not about the title or the status; it's about the trust they've placed in me to be a part of their professional network. That's a daily reminder of how far I've come and how much LinkedIn has shaped my professional journey.

For me, LinkedIn has become more than just a platform—it's a source of energy and inspiration. It fuels my drive to keep growing, keep learning, and keep expanding my network. Every time I log in, I see new opportunities, new ideas, and new possibilities. It's an endless source of motivation. That's why I always say, "Network is my net worth." It's not just a catchy phrase; it's a truth that I live by. The connections I've built, the relationships I've nurtured, and the trust I've earned on LinkedIn have become the foundation of my professional success.

What I've Learned

One of the key lessons I've learned over the years is the importance of consistency. Building a strong LinkedIn presence doesn't happen overnight. It takes time, effort, and a lot of persistence. There were times when I felt like giving up, when my posts weren't getting the traction, I hoped for, or when my connection requests went unanswered. But I kept going because I knew that the effort I was putting in would pay off in the long run.

Consistency is everything. It's not enough to post once in a while or to engage sporadically. You need to show up regularly and provide value every time. Whether it's through sharing insightful content, commenting on other people's posts, or simply reaching out to someone with a thoughtful message, every action you take on LinkedIn should be intentional. Over time, these small actions add up and lead to bigger opportunities.

Another important lesson is to be authentic. People can sense when you're being genuine and when you're just trying to sell something or promote yourself. Authenticity builds trust, and trust is the currency of LinkedIn. When I started sharing my personal stories and experiences—both the successes and the failures—that's when I saw real engagement. People connect with people, not with faceless profiles or companies.

Advice for Others

If there's one piece of advice I could give to every professional out there, it's this: take LinkedIn seriously and start early. Don't waste time on other social media platforms that drain your energy and offer little in return. Focus on building your LinkedIn network because that's where the real opportunities lie. LinkedIn isn't just for job seekers or recruiters—it's for anyone who wants to grow, learn, and connect with like-minded professionals.

The time you invest in LinkedIn today will pay off tenfold in the years to come. It's not just about landing a job or getting more clients. It's about establishing yourself as a thought leader, building meaningful relationships, and creating a network of people who will support you throughout your career. The earlier you start, the more you'll benefit in the long run.

The Turning Point in My Life

For me, LinkedIn has been the turning point in my life. It's given me more than I could have ever imagined. I've connected with people I would never have met otherwise. I've learned from the best in my industry and beyond. I've been exposed to new ideas, new opportunities, and new ways of thinking. Most importantly, LinkedIn has taught me the value of relationships and the importance of giving before you expect to receive.

So, if you're not already on LinkedIn, or if you haven't been using it to its full potential, I urge you to start today. You never know what doors it might open for you. There's a whole world of opportunity waiting, and LinkedIn is your key to unlocking it.

Take that first step. Build your profile, start connecting, and share your voice. You'll be amazed at what's possible when you tap into the power of LinkedIn. It's more than just a platform—it's your gateway to a future filled with opportunities.

Punch line - "Connect – Reflect – Direct: Power Up with LinkedIn."

Value 26 - From Connection to Conversation: How LinkedIn Built My Global Network

It was an ordinary day, just like any other, until a notification popped up on my LinkedIn. The message was brief but intriguing, an invitation to connect from one of the most high-profile professionals I had come across on the platform. I clicked on his profile out of curiosity, and there it was—his title. He was a senior leader at a well-known brand in Germany. To say I was shocked would be an understatement. This was someone whose achievements and professional standing were beyond impressive.

Without a second thought, I accepted his invitation. A few minutes later, another message arrived, asking if we could have a quick online video call. My heart raced. Why would someone at his level want to talk to me? But I decided to go with the flow, and soon, we were face-to-face on a video call.

As soon as the call started, he greeted me warmly. His demeanour was friendly, approachable, and far from what I imagined a senior executive would be. "Thank you for accepting my connection request," he said with a smile. "I've been following your LinkedIn profile for a while, and I must say, your network and followers are truly impressive."

I was still in disbelief. Here was someone who had led major projects in Germany, someone with years of experience and a vast professional network, taking the time to talk to me about my LinkedIn presence. It was surreal. He continued, "The reason for this call is simple—I want to understand how you managed to build such a massive and high-quality following on LinkedIn.

I've been told that social media can be addictive and even harmful to one's professional life. But it seems like you've found a way to make it work for you. How much time do you spend on it?"

I could tell this wasn't just a casual conversation for him. He was genuinely interested in knowing my approach to LinkedIn. I took a deep breath and started sharing my journey.

"I created my LinkedIn account back in 2012," I began, "but I wasn't active on it for the first three years. At that time, I didn't really see its potential. It wasn't until around 2015 that I realized LinkedIn could be my strength for the future. I started noticing that LinkedIn is different from other social media platforms—it's a place where real professionals engage, where people take their careers seriously. That's when I decided to give it my full attention."

He nodded, listening intently, which encouraged me to continue. "One of the things I realized early on is that LinkedIn is an organic platform. Unlike other social media sites, it doesn't push ads in your face or ask you to pay for boosting your content. The people who engage on LinkedIn are doing so because they want to, not because an algorithm is forcing it in front of them. And you know, it's interesting—whenever someone posts something political, religious, or just too personal, they get immediate feedback from the community, saying 'This isn't Facebook or Instagram; be professional.' That made me understand the power of LinkedIn as a professional tool, and I started taking it seriously from then on."

He smiled, clearly amused by the idea that LinkedIn had its own set of unwritten rules about professionalism. "So, you would say that's what sets LinkedIn apart?" he asked.

"Exactly," I said. "From 2015 onward, I dedicated myself to building my profile and my network, but it didn't happen overnight. It took about seven to eight years of consistent effort. I learned everything by experimenting with the LinkedIn algorithm. I had a full-time job, so I didn't have the luxury of spending hours on it every day. But I made the most of my weekends and holidays, dedicating those days to my LinkedIn growth."

His expression changed—he seemed to be thinking deeply about what I said. "So, you didn't have a shortcut?" he asked.

"No shortcuts," I replied. "Building a genuine, meaningful network takes time. And that's something I tell all professionals who want to build their personal brand. If you're under 30, go ahead, enjoy your social life. Watch movies, chat with friends, travel—do all the things that help you relax and have fun. But after you cross 30, you need to start thinking long-term. That's when it's time to get serious about building your brand. The time you spend hanging out with friends who don't add value to your professional growth could be better spent attending webinars, networking, and building relationships that matter."

He leaned back in his chair, nodding thoughtfully. "That's great advice," he said. "But what about social media being addictive? Don't you think people get too caught up in it?"

"That's true for platforms like Facebook or Instagram," I said. "They're designed to keep you hooked with endless entertainment. But LinkedIn is different. When I'm on LinkedIn, I feel like I'm using my time productively. I'm not scrolling mindlessly—I'm networking with people from all over the world, discussing important topics, and staying motivated. Facebook, movies, and web series drain your energy and time. They even drain your money. But when you spend your time on

LinkedIn, especially as a professional, you're investing in your future."

He seemed to appreciate the distinction I made between platforms. "So, how do you spend your time on LinkedIn? Do you invest in any paid content or courses?" he asked.

"Not really," I said. "I do attend paid webinars from time to time, but I don't pay for the expensive courses. The influencers who sell these courses often hold back critical information unless you pay for their premium content. My advice is to attend their webinars, which usually cost less than 100 INR, and absorb as much as you can from those sessions. Even if you only implement 20% of what you learn, it'll make a difference. Just be careful not to get caught up in spending too much money on courses that promise the world but don't deliver much value."

He laughed at that. "Good point! And what about recommendations? I've noticed you have quite a few on your profile."

"Yes, recommendations are another important aspect," I said. "I asked my previous managers and colleagues to write recommendations for me, and they were kind enough to do so. I have around 18 recommendations now, and they're all from reputable professionals. Having those endorsements on your profile adds credibility—it shows that people who have worked with you trust you and value your skills."

He was impressed. "So, what's the secret to building a strong network? Is it just about getting as many followers as possible?"

I shook my head. "Not at all. It's not about the number of followers—it's about the quality. You need to connect with people who add value to your professional journey. I've seen top professionals who have fewer than 5,000 followers, but those followers are all people who matter. They're leaders, decision-makers, people who can offer real insights and opportunities. So, it's not about quantity; it's about quality."

The conversation lasted for nearly an hour, and by the end of it, I could see that he was genuinely intrigued by my approach to LinkedIn. Before we ended the call, he thanked me once again for my time and said that he had a lot to think about. I, on the other hand, was still trying to process the fact that someone of his stature had reached out to me for advice. It was a humbling experience, and one that reminded me of the power of perseverance and the importance of building something authentic.

As I logged off, I realized that this was just the beginning. There would be more conversations, more opportunities, and more growth. LinkedIn had opened doors for me that I never imagined, and I knew that if I continued to invest my time and energy into it, there would be no limit to what I could achieve.

Punch Line: "Link, Think, and Watch Your Network Grow in a Blink!"

Value 27 - The Journey of Helping Others Find Jobs

Back in early 2014, I began something small, something so simple that I never imagined it would grow into a movement. Today, that small action has turned into a thriving network of over 10,000 members across various WhatsApp and Telegram groups, all aimed at one purpose—helping people find jobs. But the truth is, I never had a grand plan when I started this. I didn't set out with a blueprint or strategy; instead, it began with two powerful encounters that changed how I saw the world and my role in it.

The First Encounter: The Young Man on the Train

One day, as I was traveling on a train, something unusual happened. I was minding my own business, lost in my thoughts, when a young man entered the compartment. His face was a mix of frustration and disappointment. He carried a stack of certificates and medals, clearly the marks of his academic achievements. He was a fresh double graduate, which by all measures should have been a source of pride for him. But instead of joy, all I saw in his eyes was despair.

The young man began going from passenger to passenger, pleading for help. He showed his degrees to anyone who would listen, explaining how, despite his qualifications, he had been jobless for over a year. His frustration was obvious, and the disappointment in his voice hit me hard. He spoke about how our education system had failed him—how after spending lakhs on his education, there was still no job for him.

The scene was heartbreaking. Here was someone who had done everything right, followed the system, earned the degrees, but was left with nothing to show for it. His desperation was real, and it was in front of everyone to see. As I watched him, a thought occurred to me: the passengers on that train, the people he was pleading with, they weren't the right audience for his cry for help. These were regular folks, probably traveling by train to save money. They weren't employers or people with the right connections.

It was clear that while his approach was sincere, it was misplaced. This young man was asking for help, but from the wrong people. That moment was a revelation for me. It made me realize the importance of targeting the right audience, especially when you need help. This idea stuck with me and became one of the major reasons why I started focusing on building a professional network on LinkedIn. It wasn't enough to just want a job; you had to know where to look and who to ask.

The Second Encounter: A Friend in Despair

The second encounter that changed my perspective was far more personal. It involved one of my close friends. He was a talented individual, someone I admired greatly, but one day he lost his job due to internal politics at his company. For six long months, he was without work. At first, he tried to stay positive, but slowly, the reality of his situation began to weigh him down.

Being jobless affected more than just his financial situation; it chipped away at his confidence, his sense of self-worth. Worse, his family began to humiliate him for not being able to provide. His once-bright outlook on life darkened. The pressure became unbearable, and my friend began to sink into despair.

Then, one evening, something happened that I'll never forget. By sheer luck—or perhaps it was divine intervention—I decided to call him. His voice was distant, hollow, as if he was barely holding on. As we talked, he confessed something that shook me to my core: he had been seriously contemplating ending his life. The joblessness, the humiliation, the weight of his own expectations—all of it had pushed him to the brink. He was only hours away from making a decision that would have been irreversible.

I felt a chill run through me. I couldn't believe what I was hearing. I promised him right there that I would do everything in my power to help him find a job. And I did. Over the next few weeks, I pulled every string, contacted every person I could, and in the end, I managed to help him secure a position. But that experience left a mark on me that I couldn't shake.

It opened my eyes to just how deeply joblessness can affect a person. It wasn't just about the money—it was about dignity, purpose, and self-respect. I realized that while giving someone financial support could help them for a day, helping them find a job could change their entire future. It was like the old saying: "Don't give a man a fish; teach him how to fish."

The Birth of a Movement

These two incidents—the young man on the train and my friend's near-tragic experience—planted the seeds for what would eventually grow into a much larger initiative. At first, I didn't have a clear plan. I just knew that I wanted to help. I started by creating small WhatsApp groups where people could share job openings, offer advice, and support each other. It was a humble beginning, but it was something.

To my surprise, the groups started to grow quickly. Word spread, and soon enough, more people wanted to join. What began as a small initiative transformed into a network that now spans over 10,000 members across various WhatsApp and Telegram groups. Every day, job seekers share leads, tips, and advice, helping each other in ways that go beyond just finding work. The sense of community is incredible, and it's a testament to how powerful it is when people come together with a common purpose.

Helping People Regain Hope

Looking back at everything we've built; I realize that this initiative is about much more than just helping people find jobs. It's about giving people back their confidence, their dignity, and their sense of purpose. It's about showing them that they're not alone, that there's a community of people who understand their struggles and are willing to help.

For many, being jobless can feel like the end of the road, but it doesn't have to be. Through these groups, I've seen countless stories of people who were at their lowest point, feeling lost and hopeless, but who found new opportunities and regained their sense of worth. It's a powerful reminder that, sometimes, the smallest actions—like creating a WhatsApp group—can have the most profound impact.

A Lifelong Lesson

The journey has taught me a lifelong lesson: never underestimate the power of community. In a world that often feels disconnected, where it's easy to feel like you're facing your struggles alone, building a network of support can make all the difference. It's not about grand gestures or massive initiatives; sometimes, it's about small, consistent efforts that create a ripple effect.

I'm proud of what we've accomplished, not just because of the numbers or the success stories, but because of the hope we've restored in people's lives. For every person who finds a job through these groups, there's a ripple effect that goes far beyond the individual. Their families, their communities, and their futures are impacted. That's what makes this work so meaningful.

Punch Line: "From Train Rides to Saving Lives, Job Help Thrives Where Hope Survives"

As I reflect on this journey, it's amazing to think that it all started with a train ride and a phone call that, quite literally, saved a life. What began as a simple idea has turned into a thriving network of people helping each other find jobs and rebuild their lives. And at the heart of it all is one simple truth: job help thrives where hope survives.

Value 28 - The Other Side of Helping—Letting Go of Expectations

Helping people find jobs has been one of the most rewarding experiences of my life. Over the years, I've been able to assist hundreds of individuals, many of whom might not have had much of a chance without some support. Based on the feedback I've received, I estimate that I've directly helped around 200 to 250 people secure jobs, while indirectly, that number likely exceeds 500. But as fulfilling as it is to see someone land a job and regain their sense of purpose, I've also come to realize that helping has its own side effects, ones that I wasn't prepared for when I first started this journey.

What surprised me the most wasn't the joy that came from helping others—it was the reaction, or lack of reaction, from those I had helped once their problem was solved. At first, I thought my role in their lives would remain significant, that perhaps I'd made a lasting impact. But I quickly learned that wasn't always the case.

The Disappearing Act:

One of the most unexpected realities I faced was how quickly many people seemed to move on after getting the help they needed. I remember vividly the first few times it happened. After spending weeks, sometimes months, helping someone with job leads, preparing their resume, coaching them through interviews, and eventually celebrating their success, they'd suddenly vanish. The phone calls stopped, the messages dried up, and soon, it felt like I was forgotten.

At first, I chalked it up to people getting busy with their new jobs, which, of course, made sense. But as it happened again and again, I realized that a significant number of the people I helped—about 60% by my estimation—never really looked back. They didn't reach out just to check in or even say thank you after a while. It was as if, once their struggle was over, their connection to me no longer served a purpose. And while I never helped anyone expecting grand gestures or lifelong friendships, the lack of acknowledgment stung.

It wasn't just a one-off occurrence either. It became a pattern. Time and time again, I would offer my assistance, pouring my energy and effort into helping someone land on their feet, only to watch them drift away once they were back on solid ground. Each time it happened, I found myself wondering if I had done something wrong or if maybe I had misjudged the impact I was making. It felt disheartening, and I couldn't help but feel a bit used. It was as if my support had been valuable only as long as it was needed, and after that, I was simply discarded.

Coming to Terms with Reality:

These experiences gradually began to shape my mindset. I started to realize that when you help someone, you shouldn't expect anything in return—not even gratitude. It's a hard pill to swallow, especially when you've put so much heart into helping someone through a tough time. But expecting acknowledgment, recognition, or even just a friendly follow-up only leads to disappointment.

The truth is, people are often so caught up in their own lives, especially after overcoming a difficult period, that they forget to look back and appreciate those who helped them along the way. It's not necessarily out of malice or ingratitude, but more because life moves fast, and once they've solved their problem, they shift their focus to what comes next. I had to learn that, in many cases, people aren't intentionally forgetting; they're simply moving on.

As I reflected on this, I started to see my role in a different light. It dawned on me that it wasn't really me who was doing the helping. I came to believe that I was simply a vessel, a tool through which something greater—God, the universe, fate, whatever you want to call it—was working. I wasn't the solution; I was just part of the process.

Once I adopted this mindset, I felt an immense sense of relief. The pressure to be remembered or thanked began to fade away. The disappointment I felt when people didn't reach out again started to dissolve. It was like a weight being lifted from my shoulders. I realized that my reward wasn't in the thank you or the lasting relationships—it was in the act of helping itself. Just knowing that I had played a part, however small, in someone's success was enough.

Expectations Hurt:

There's a saying that has stuck with me throughout this journey: "Expectations hurt." And it's true, more than I ever realized before. When you expect something from others, whether it's gratitude, acknowledgment, or even just a message to see how you're doing, you set yourself up for disappointment. People aren't always going to respond the way you want them to. They have their own lives, their own priorities, and sometimes, they don't have the bandwidth to look back and offer thanks.

But here's the thing—when you stop expecting, you set yourself free. Free from disappointment, free from frustration, and free from the hurt that comes from feeling unappreciated. This shift in perspective was a game-changer for me. It brought me a sense of peace that I hadn't experienced before. I still help people whenever I can, but now I do it with no strings attached, no expectations of anything in return. I help for the sake of helping, and that alone is enough.

This lesson has changed the way I approach not just helping others, but life in general. I no longer feel the need for recognition or acknowledgment. I've come to understand that the greatest reward is the inner satisfaction that comes from knowing you did something good, even if no one else notices. And that's more than enough.

Finding Freedom in Letting Go:

One of the most powerful realizations I've had through this process is that letting go of expectations isn't just about avoiding disappointment—it's about finding freedom. When you help someone and expect nothing in return, you free yourself from the emotional baggage that comes with unmet expectations. You help because you want to, not because you're waiting for a thank you or a favour in return. And in that, there is immense freedom.

I've come to embrace this idea fully. The people I help may never remember me, and that's okay. What matters is that I played my part. I was there when they needed help, and that's enough for me. This shift in mindset has made me happier, more content, and more at peace with the world around me.

But more than that, it's strengthened my faith. I've come to believe that everything happens for a reason, and we all have a role to play in each other's lives, even if that role is temporary or goes unacknowledged. When I help someone now, I see it as part of a bigger plan, one that I don't need to fully understand. I'm simply doing what I'm meant to do, and that's all the reward I need.

Helping for the Sake of Helping:

At the end of the day, helping others isn't about being remembered or thanked. It's about doing what you can, when you can, and finding joy in the act itself. I've come to realize that the most important thing is the intention behind the help. If your heart is in the right place, then the outcome, whether it's acknowledged or not, doesn't matter.

This mindset has allowed me to continue helping people with a lighter heart. I no longer feel disappointed when people move on and forget to express their gratitude. Instead, I focus on the positive impact I've made in the moment. I know that the real reward is the sense of fulfilment that comes from making a difference in someone's life, even if it's just a small difference.

Helping for the sake of helping has become my mantra. It's a lesson that has brought me immense peace, and it's a lesson I hope others can learn as well. Because once you let go of the need for acknowledgment, you open yourself up to a whole new world of happiness and freedom. And that, in my opinion, is the greatest gift of all.

Freedom in Selflessness

The journey of helping others has been full of highs and lows, but the most valuable lesson I've learned is that true selflessness comes from letting go of expectations. When you help without wanting anything in return, not even a thank you, you free yourself from the hurt that comes with unmet expectations. You find joy in the act itself, and that's where the real reward lies.

I've come to see that my role in helping others isn't about being recognized; it's about being part of a larger plan, one that I may never fully understand. And that's okay. Helping for the sake of helping, without expecting anything in return, has brought me peace, strengthened my faith, and given me a sense of freedom that I never knew before. And in the end, that freedom is the greatest gift I could ever ask for.

Punch Line: "Help with no strings, and peace is what it brings"

Value 29 - The Art of Controlled Aggressiveness

In both my personal and professional life, I've always been fascinated by the fine line between being assertive and being aggressive. It's a line we all walk at some point, but few people seem to understand how to balance the two effectively. For as long as I can remember, I've heard countless influencers, and motivational speakers advocate for assertiveness. They praise it as the ideal middle ground between being too passive and too forceful. And while I understand the appeal of assertiveness, I've found that in my experience, a different approach often yields better results: what I call controlled aggressiveness.

Now, before you jump to conclusions, let me explain what I mean by aggressiveness. It's not about being hostile or trying to dominate others. It's not about raising your voice, forcing your will, or bullying anyone into submission. Controlled aggressiveness is about being prepared, being decisive, and showing strength when necessary—without overstepping boundaries or harming anyone in the process. To help explain this idea, I often use the analogy of a sword.

The Sword at Your Side

Imagine you have a sword—a weapon of power and precision—sheathed at your side. It's there, hanging on your hip, but hidden from view. The people around you might see the hilt or the outline of the blade, but they don't know for sure if you'll ever draw it. They may underestimate you, assuming you'll never use it. They might feel emboldened to challenge you, thinking they can push your limits because they believe you'll never react.

This is where the first level of controlled aggressiveness comes into play. You unsheathe your sword, not to strike, but to show that you're capable of doing so. You let others see that you possess the power and that you're not afraid to reveal your strength when the situation calls for it. This act alone can often deter potential challenges. It's a subtle but powerful message: "I'm prepared, and I won't hesitate to defend myself or what I believe in."

This step in controlled aggressiveness is important because it allows you to assert your position without escalating to unnecessary conflict. By simply showing that you're ready and willing to stand your ground, you often prevent issues before they even arise.

Demonstrating Your Skill

But there are times when just showing the sword isn't enough. Some people may still doubt your resolve. They might think you're bluffing, that your display of strength is nothing more than a façade. These are the moments when you need to take it a step further.

In these situations, I demonstrate my skill with the sword. I don't just show it—I swing it through the air, letting others see that I know how to use it. I might not use it to harm, but I make it clear that I'm not just carrying it for show. I'm capable. I'm competent. This is the second level of controlled aggressiveness: proving that you're not only willing to act, but that you know how to act effectively.

In business, this might look like clearly stating your boundaries in a negotiation, demonstrating your expertise, or laying out the consequences of an unfair deal. In personal relationships, it could mean standing firm on something that's important to you, making it clear that you won't be swayed or taken advantage of.

It's about proving that you're not afraid to use the tools at your disposal to protect your interests.

Even then, though, there will always be those who want to evaluate you further. People who refuse to take you seriously until they're faced with the reality of your resolve.

The Blade at the Throat

When someone still refuses to back down, even after seeing your strength, that's when you have to advance. You move forward, sword in hand, and place it at their throat. This is the third level of controlled aggressiveness—showing that you're willing to go as far as necessary to defend your position or protect your interests. The blade at their neck is a clear signal: "I'm serious, and I'm not afraid to act."

In practical terms, this might mean delivering a final ultimatum in a negotiation or taking a firm, decisive action that leaves no room for misinterpretation. It's the moment when you've tried to warn others, but they didn't listen—so now you're showing them exactly how far you're willing to go.

But here's where the key to controlled aggressiveness comes into play: I never cut. No matter how far the situation escalates, I never actually harm anyone or cross the line into irreversible actions. Because while it's important to show strength, it's equally important to maintain control. If I were to cut, to actually use the sword in a harmful way, I'd be committing a crime—not just in a literal sense, but in a moral sense as well. I'd be overstepping, damaging relationships, or causing harm that I can't undo.

Controlled aggressiveness is about walking that tightrope between power and restraint. It's about knowing how to assert yourself without tipping into aggression that leads to negative consequences. This balance requires confidence, but more importantly, it requires discipline.

Finding the Balance

This approach has served me well in both business and personal life. In business, it's helped me negotiate better deals, stand firm in difficult situations, and earn respect from colleagues and competitors alike. People know that I'm prepared, that I know my worth, and that I won't back down when it matters. But they also know that I won't act recklessly or unnecessarily escalate a situation. It's a fine balance, but one that garners respect and results.

In my personal life, controlled aggressiveness has helped me set boundaries and protect the things that matter to me. Whether it's standing up for my values or ensuring that I'm not taken advantage of in relationships, this approach has allowed me to maintain my integrity while also avoiding unnecessary conflicts.

There have been moments when people have tried to push me past my limits, but by showing them my "sword"—by being assertive yet controlled—I've been able to navigate those challenges without crossing any dangerous lines. The key is that I never overreact, never let my emotions take over, and never use more force than is necessary.

By showing that I have the sword and that I know how to use it, I've been able to move through life with a sense of purpose and direction. But by never actually cutting, I've maintained my integrity, avoided unnecessary conflicts, and preserved important relationships. This, to me, is the true essence of controlled aggressiveness: the ability to be strong and assertive, without ever crossing the line into harmful behaviour.

The Sword Stays Sheathed

At the end of the day, controlled aggressiveness isn't about overpowering others or proving your strength through force. It's about understanding your own power, using it wisely, and knowing when to draw the sword—and when to keep it sheathed. It's about being prepared to defend yourself and your interests, but never acting impulsively or without thought.

This approach requires a deep understanding of yourself and the situations you find yourself in. You have to be willing to show your strength, but you also have to know when to hold back. It's not about dominance or aggression for aggression's sake. It's about calculated action, about asserting yourself in a way that is both firm and fair.

In life, there will always be moments when you need to stand up for yourself or for what you believe in. And in those moments, it's important to have the sword at your side—ready but restrained. Knowing that you have the ability to act is often enough to prevent conflicts from escalating. But knowing when not to act is what separates controlled aggressiveness from reckless aggression.

The Power of Restraint

As I've navigated the challenges of both my personal and professional life, I've learned that controlled aggressiveness is a valuable tool. It's allowed me to assert myself, when necessary, protect my interests, and earn respect from those around me. But the true power of this approach lies in its restraint.

By showing strength without crossing the line into aggression, I've been able to maintain control, avoid unnecessary conflicts, and preserve important relationships. I've learned that the real art of controlled aggressiveness is knowing when to draw the sword—and when to keep it sheathed.

So, when it comes to navigating the fine line between assertiveness and aggression, my advice is simple: don't be afraid to show your strength, but always remember that true power lies in knowing when not to use it.

Punch line "Show your might, but keep it tight; wield the sword, yet spare the fight."

Value 30 - The Relay Race That Changed My Perspective on Teamwork

I was 28 or 29 years old when I found myself standing at the edge of a track field, watching a relay race that would unknowingly shape my understanding of teamwork forever. It was a state-level competition, and the atmosphere was electric. Talented athletes, each with their own dreams and ambitions, were warming up, ready to give their all for their teams. As I observed the runners stretching, focused and determined, I felt a sense of excitement. But what I didn't realize at the time was that this race would teach me a lesson far beyond what I had learned in my professional life.

At that point in my career, I was struggling to manage teams effectively. Despite all the motivational talks I'd listened to, the leadership books I'd read, and the countless theories on teamwork I'd absorbed, something wasn't clicking. I knew teamwork was crucial, but the concept felt elusive and abstract. It was easy to understand in theory, but difficult to apply in real-world situations. I tried different strategies—team-building exercises, one-on-one meetings, giving pep talks—but it all felt forced. I couldn't shake the feeling that I was missing something fundamental.

That was, until I witnessed this race.

The Relay Race Begins:

The relay race was 2000 meters long, with each team consisting of four to five runners. Each athlete had to complete a leg of 400 to 500 meters, carrying a baton that they would pass on to the next runner. The race itself seemed simple: run your part, hand over the baton, and trust your teammate to continue the race. But what I didn't realize then was that this simple race was a reflection of the dynamics of teamwork, and the lessons it held would change the way I thought about leading teams.

As the races began, I stood on the sidelines, watching intently. The first match was particularly memorable. The starting gun fired, and the first runner shot out like a bullet, setting an impressive pace. His speed was astonishing, and I was sure his team had the race in the bag. But when it came time to pass the baton to the final runner, something unexpected happened. The last runner, though eager, struggled to maintain the speed set by his teammate. He lagged behind, and despite the strong start, the team ended up losing the race.

It was a jarring sight. One person's incredible effort wasn't enough to secure a win. I couldn't help but think, what if the baton had been passed differently? What if the team had balanced their efforts better?

The Unexpected Victory:

In the next race, I witnessed something entirely different. This time, the first three runners weren't particularly fast. In fact, they seemed to be lagging behind, running at a slower, more measured pace compared to the other teams. As the baton was passed from one runner to the next, I thought for sure this team was out of the race. But when the final runner got hold of the baton, everything changed. It was as if a fire had been lit within him. He sprinted with incredible speed, overtaking all the other teams to clinch victory in the final moments of the race.

The crowd erupted in cheers, but I stood there, stunned. This race had unfolded in a way I hadn't expected. How could a team that had started so slowly end up winning in the end? Who was responsible for their victory? Was it the last runner who sprinted so brilliantly, or was it the earlier runners who conserved their energy and stayed steady?

As I thought about it, the answer became clear: it wasn't any one person who was responsible. It was the team as a whole. Each runner played their part, even if it didn't seem impressive at first. The final runner may have secured the win, but the earlier runners had kept the team in the race. The victory belonged to all of them.

A New Understanding of Teamwork:

That race was a revelation for me. For the first time, I saw teamwork in a new light. In a relay race, no single runner can win the race alone. Every runner contributes, and the baton—the symbol of trust—must be passed from one to the other with care. It's not about individual glory; it's about the collective effort to achieve a common goal. And this, I realized, is true not only on the track but in every team, in every aspect of life.

I started to think about the teams I had managed over the years, and I began to see where I had gone wrong. I had been focusing too much on individual performance. I wanted each team member to shine, but in doing so, I had lost sight of the bigger picture. I hadn't fostered a true sense of shared responsibility. I was managing individuals instead of building a team.

Watching that relay race, I realized that teamwork isn't just about delegating tasks or motivating individuals; it's about creating an environment where everyone understands their role and supports one another. It's about trusting your teammates to carry the baton when it's their turn and being ready to take it when it's yours. And most importantly, it's about the understanding that no one person can win alone.

The Importance of Trust:

In a relay race, the baton is passed from one runner to the next, but it's not just a physical handoff—it's a transfer of trust. When you pass the baton, you trust that the next person will continue the race with the same effort and commitment that you did. And when you receive the baton, you take on the responsibility to carry it forward.

This, I realized, is the essence of teamwork. It's not enough to just do your part; you must trust your teammates to do theirs, too. Without that trust, the team falls apart. In the professional world, this means creating an environment where team members feel confident in each other's abilities and are willing to rely on one another.

Too often, I had seen teams fail because they didn't trust each other. People would try to do everything themselves, thinking that if they didn't, the project would fail. But that's not how teams succeed. Teams succeed when everyone works together, when each person understands that they are part of something bigger than themselves. When you pass the baton, you're saying, "I trust you," and when you receive it, you're saying, "I've got this."

Applying the Lesson in Life and Work:

That day, standing at the edge of the track, I learned a lesson that would become a cornerstone of how I approach teamwork in every aspect of my life. It wasn't just about managing teams at work; it was about understanding that in any group effort—whether it's a family, a workplace, or even a group of friends—

everyone has a role to play, and the success of the group depends on each person doing their part.

When I returned to work, I began to apply what I had learned. Instead of focusing on individual performance, I started fostering a sense of shared responsibility. I encouraged team members to support one another, to pass the baton when needed, and to trust that their teammates would carry it forward. It wasn't easy at first—old habits die hard—but gradually, I saw a shift in the way my teams operated. They started working together more cohesively, and the results were clear: better performance, stronger relationships, and a more positive work environment.

The most important change, though, was in me. I stopped trying to control everything. I stopped worrying about individual success and started focusing on the team as a whole. I realized that leadership isn't about being the fastest runner; it's about knowing when to pass the baton and trusting that your team will carry it to the finish line.

The relay race taught me that true teamwork is about more than just individual effort—it's about working together, trusting each other, and understanding that success is a shared journey. Whether on the track, at work, or in life, the goal isn't to shine alone but to win together.

Each person's role, no matter how big or small, contributes to the team's success. And when we pass the baton—whether it's in a project, a challenge, or an opportunity—we're not just handing over responsibility; we're sharing trust and ensuring that together, we'll cross the finish line. The victory is not won by any single person but by the entire team working in unison. And that, to me, is the true essence of teamwork.

Punch Line: "Pass the Baton, Share the Pace; Together We Win, Together We Race"

Value 31 - Triumph Over Back Pain

It was around the age of 29 when I faced one of the toughest battles of my life—this one wasn't in the boardroom or a workplace, but within my own body. Years of riding my bike on rough, unforgiving roads had taken their toll, and the consequences caught up with me in a way I never anticipated. My lower back—specifically, the L4 and L5 discs—had become dislocated. What followed was an experience I wouldn't wish on anyone: the excruciating, relentless pain of sciatica.

Sciatica, in my opinion, is one of the worst pains a person can endure. When those dislocated discs compressed my sciatic nerve, it felt like a lightning bolt tearing through my body. The pain was so sharp and intense that it could strike me down on the spot, leaving me unable to move, frozen in whatever position I had collapsed into. The pain was like an electric shock, so powerful that it seemed to bypass my body and shoot straight to my brain, overwhelming all other senses.

Even something as simple as getting to bed became a struggle. I could only lie in one specific position, and even that offered little comfort. Every night was a battle, trying to find a posture that didn't send another bolt of pain shooting through my back. The pain would strike unpredictably—whether I was walking, sitting, or just trying to go about my day. Sometimes, the dislocated discs would shift just enough to press on the nerve again, sending me into agony. It was like walking on a tightrope, never knowing when the next step would trigger that unbearable pain.

The Diagnosis and a Tough Choice

After months of enduring this torment, I knew I couldn't put off seeing a doctor any longer. It wasn't just affecting my work; it was taking over my life. A series of scans confirmed what I had suspected but dreaded: the condition was in its final stages. The doctor recommended surgery to replace the damaged discs, but the prospect didn't offer me any relief.

I didn't take the decision to avoid surgery lightly. I spoke with several people who had undergone similar surgeries, and their experiences were discouraging. Many of them were still dealing with pain, even after the procedure, and some faced complications that made their situation worse. The thought of going through surgery only to end up in the same—or an even worse—state terrified me. That's when I made a decision that would change the course of my life: I was going to fight this battle without surgery.

The Fight Begins

The next few months were some of the hardest I've ever faced. The pain didn't subside just because I had made up my mind to avoid surgery. If anything, it felt even more relentless. Every day was a test of my endurance. Simple tasks became almost impossible, and every movement was accompanied by the fear that the pain might strike again. But I had made my decision, and I was determined to see it through.

I started with physiotherapy, undergoing countless sessions to try and strengthen my back and ease the pressure on the discs. I wore a back support belt for months to alleviate some of the strain and tried every conventional treatment I could find. Despite all these efforts, the improvement was slow and minimal. The pain still loomed large over my life, and there were days when I wondered if I had made a mistake by rejecting surgery.

Then, as a last resort, I turned to naturopathy. This was something I had never considered before, but I was willing to try anything. Naturopathy focuses on natural remedies and therapies, and although I was sceptical at first, it gradually began to make a difference. The treatment wasn't a miracle cure by any means. It didn't take the pain away overnight, but over time, I started to feel subtle improvements. Combined with my determination to fight, it slowly became clear that this approach might work.

Four Years of Battle

I wish I could say that my recovery happened quickly, but it didn't. It took four long years of struggle—years filled with pain, frustration, and countless moments when I wanted to give up. I was constantly juggling physiotherapy, naturopathy, and everyday life, which was still punctuated by sharp bouts of pain. The mental toll was just as hard as the physical one. Sciatica can make you feel helpless, but I knew I couldn't give in to that feeling.

During these years, my daily life was about managing the pain as much as it was about moving forward. The support of family and friends was essential, but so was my own stubbornness. I refused to let this condition control my life, and slowly, the hard work started to pay off.

Gradually, the pain began to lessen. I noticed that the electric shocks shooting through my back weren't as frequent, and when they did come, they weren't as severe. The healing was incremental, but it was there. Step by step, I was regaining control over my body. I started feeling stronger, more resilient, and more in command of my health.

The Victory Over Sciatica

After four long years, I finally won the battle against sciatica. It wasn't a moment of triumph that happened all at once, but a gradual realization that I had come out on the other side. The pain that had once ruled my life was now something I had overcome. I could move freely again, without the constant fear of that sharp, debilitating shock of pain hitting me out of nowhere.

But this victory wasn't just about overcoming sciatica. It was about proving something to myself. I had chosen a difficult path—the path without surgery—and fought through the pain with sheer determination. This experience gave me a newfound confidence. It showed me that I had the strength and resilience to tackle even the most daunting challenges. If I could fight through four years of pain and come out stronger, I knew I could face anything that life threw at me.

Looking back, this battle wasn't just a physical one—it was a mental and emotional test as well. There were moments when I wanted to give up, when the pain felt too overwhelming, but I didn't. Every day, I took it one step at a time, focusing not on the final outcome but on getting through the next challenge, no matter how small. And that's how I won. I didn't overcome sciatica in one heroic act. I beat it by surviving the daily grind, by refusing to let it define me.

Lessons Learned

My battle with sciatica taught me more than just how to manage pain—it taught me valuable life lessons. I learned the importance of patience and persistence. Healing, whether physical or emotional, doesn't happen overnight. It takes time, sometimes much longer than we expect. But if you stay committed, even when the progress is slow, you can get through it.

I also learned that it's okay to try different approaches to solving a problem. When conventional methods didn't work for me, I turned to naturopathy, something I had never considered before. Sometimes, the path to recovery isn't linear, and you have to be open to exploring new ideas and treatments. What worked for someone else might not work for you, and that's okay. It's about finding what works for you personally.

Finally, this experience taught me to never underestimate the power of your own will. There will be moments in life when you feel completely powerless, but those are the moments when your inner strength is evaluated. If you dig deep enough, you'll find that you're capable of more than you think.

Moving Forward

Today, I'm stronger, both physically and mentally, because of what I went through with sciatica. It wasn't a challenge I chose, but it was one that shaped me. I'm grateful for the lessons it taught me and the resilience it helped me build. Now, when I face challenges in my professional or personal life, I remind myself of the battle I fought and won against my own body. If I could get through that, I can get through anything.

In the end, this battle wasn't just about beating sciatica. It was about proving to myself that no matter how tough things get, with enough dedication, belief, and perseverance, I can overcome any obstacle.

Punch line - "Beat the Pain, Rise Again—Strength is My Gain!"

Value 32 - The Journey to Financial Freedom

One of the biggest regrets of my life was realizing how late I came to understand the concept of financial freedom. It wasn't until I was well into my 30s that I even heard the term. But as I started diving into the world of money management, I quickly discovered that this isn't just my problem—it's an issue faced by the majority of India's youth. Our education system simply doesn't teach us about real money management.

Growing up, my parents taught us to save money. The lesson was simple: if I earned 100 rupees, I should save 20 of it. For the longest time, I believed that was the path to financial security. But as I got older, I realized that it's not just about saving money; it's about growing it.

Social media played a huge role in my financial education. I started watching YouTube videos and attending webinars that introduced me to systematic investments, the stock market, and mutual funds—concepts I had never encountered before. Before this, my understanding of investing was limited to gold, real estate, LIC policies, and fixed deposits—traditional options that were passed down from my parents.

One of the key messages I share during my talks now is a plea to the younger generation, even college students, to start investing early. I always emphasize the power of starting small, like investing your pocket money in a mutual fund and setting up a monthly SIP (Systematic Investment Plan). The most fascinating concept I came across was the "magic of compounding."

The magic of compounding blew my mind when I first learned about it. I remember hearing the story about a chessboard, where if you place one grain of rice on the first square and then double it on each subsequent square, by the time you reach the last square, the amount of rice would be astronomical. This simple yet powerful story illustrated how small, consistent investments could grow exponentially over time. It was a game-changer for me, and it became the foundation of my approach to financial management.

One memorable experience that cemented my belief in smart investing happened when I met an old friend after a long time. When I saw him, I could hardly believe my eyes. He came from a middle-class background, but now he was decked out in branded clothes, expensive sunglasses (even though it was evening and the sun was setting), costly shoes, and a strong, high-end perfume that you could smell from a distance.

We greeted each other, and it didn't take long for him to start showing off. He pulled out a brand-new Apple iPhone, clearly waiting for me to ask about it. But instead, I kept the conversation focused on his family and other things. After a while, he couldn't resist and asked me if I had an iPhone. I smiled and said, “Yes.”

He immediately wanted to know which model I had, but I responded casually, saying, "Who remembers? They launch a new one every 8 to 10 months, and the old models quickly become obsolete."

He looked puzzled and asked what I meant. I explained, “I don't buy an iPhone as a consumer. Instead, I invest in Apple shares in the US market. That way, I become a part-owner of the company. So, when people buy iPhones, I'm happy because it means more sales, higher stock prices, and a growing net worth for me."

Then I started telling him about other investments I had made in the brands he was wearing. He was shocked when I told him about the returns I had earned. The clothes, shoes, and gadgets he was flaunting were depreciating assets. The moment he bought them, their value began to decrease. But my investments, on the other hand, were growing and increasing my net worth over time.

I've come to understand that it's far wiser to invest in appreciating assets—things that grow in value—rather than splurging on attractive branded stuff that just depreciates with time. This mindset shift was crucial for me in achieving financial freedom.

Now, whenever I think about financial freedom, I realize it's not just about having enough money to buy what you want. It's about making your money work for you, growing it, and securing your future. And the earlier you start, the more powerful the results.

This experience taught me that true wealth comes not from what you spend but from what you wisely invest. It's a message I share with everyone I can, hoping to inspire others to take control of their financial futures as well.

Now I will share an interesting interpretation of mine about who is rich? with a small story…

The Real Meaning of Rich:

It was one of those days when life teaches you something unexpected. I was at a railway station, waiting for a train that was already running late. The platform was crowded, and everyone seemed restless, including me. I had a lot of luggage with me—heavy bags that I knew would be a struggle to carry when the train finally arrived.

The sky was cloudy, but I didn't think much of it. Suddenly, without warning, the clouds burst open, and heavy rain poured down. It was as if someone had flipped a switch. The platform quickly turned chaotic. People were scrambling for shelter, trying to protect themselves and their belongings. But there was hardly any space to take cover, and with our train just two minutes away, panic started setting in.

Our compartment was at the far end of the platform, quite a distance from where we stood. There was no shelter along the way, and the rain showed no signs of stopping. I looked around, and I saw the same worry on the faces of others. We all had heavy luggage, and the thought of running through the rain to reach our compartment was daunting.

Just then, I noticed a man among us who seemed different. While the rest of us were hesitating, unsure of how to protect ourselves and our belongings, this man was fully prepared. He calmly opened up a large umbrella, the kind that could easily cover two people. He wrapped his luggage in a raincoat, ensuring it would stay dry. Then, with a confident stride, he started walking towards the train like it was just another day.

At that moment, it struck me—he was the richest person on that platform. Not because he had money or status, but because he had exactly what he needed at that precise moment. While the rest of us were struggling, caught off guard by the sudden downpour, he was fully equipped and ready to manage the situation. He had the right tools, in the right quantity, and of the right quality to get to his desired destination without worry.

That day, I realized that being rich isn't just about having money or assets. It's about having what you need when you need it most. It's about being prepared, being ready to face life's unexpected challenges with confidence. The richest person in the room isn't always the one with the most wealth; sometimes, it's the one who has the foresight and the means to handle any situation that comes their way.

As I watched him board the train with ease, while the rest of us hurriedly tried to follow, soaking wet and struggling with our luggage, I couldn't help but smile. That man wasn't just wealthy in the traditional sense—he was rich in preparation, in foresight, and in the ability to adapt. And that, I realized, is a kind of wealth that's far more valuable than money.

Punch line "Save Smart, Grow Wealth from the Start!"

"Invest to Grow, Watch Wealth Flow!"

"Richness isn't just in gold, but in the readiness, we hold!"

Value 33 - The Japanese Influence That Shaped My Life

My journey with Japan began almost by chance. Fresh out of college, I was selected for a campus placement with a reputed Indian automotive company. Little did I know at the time, but this company wasn't just another workplace; it was deeply rooted in Japanese culture and systems. From the moment I stepped into that office, I was immersed in an environment that operated with the precision, discipline, and attention to detail that Japan is known for. This early introduction to Japanese principles would eventually become the bedrock of my professional journey and, later, my personal philosophy.

I was introduced to concepts like Kaizen (continuous improvement), 5S (sort, set in order, shine, standardize, sustain), and lean manufacturing—terms that at first sounded like corporate jargon, but soon proved to be much more. These weren't just buzzwords meant to impress clients or upper management. They were a way of life at the company, lived and breathed by every employee, every day. Slowly, without even realizing it, I started adopting these practices. I began to see the world through a different lens—a Japanese lens—where everything was about improving, finding efficiency, and maintaining a standard of excellence in both work and daily life.

I started organizing my personal space with the 5S principles, trying to find small improvements in my daily routine with Kaizen, and constantly striving for efficiency. It wasn't just about being better at work—it was about making every part of my life flow more smoothly. The more I immersed myself in these principles, the more I admired the philosophy behind them.

But it wasn't until I had the opportunity to visit Japan that I truly understood the depth of this connection.

A Journey to Japan

My first trip to Japan wasn't just a professional visit—it was a personal revelation. The moment I arrived, I was struck by the country's seamless blend of tradition and modernity. I had read about this balance but seeing it with my own eyes was something else entirely. Japan honoured its rich cultural heritage while embracing cutting-edge technology with ease. In Tokyo, towering skyscrapers stood next to centuries-old temples, and in every corner of the city, you could see how respect for the past coexisted harmoniously with the future.

Everything in Japan worked with a level of precision that left me in awe. The streets were clean, the people were polite, and there was a quiet sense of order and discipline that I had never experienced before. Even the smallest details—like how a shopkeeper placed change in my hand or how public transport arrived in the minute—were managed with care and meticulous attention.

I began to understand that Japanese systems of efficiency and improvement weren't just corporate strategies—they were embedded into the very fabric of society. But the moment that truly changed my life came not in the bustling cities or efficient trains. It came during my visit to Hiroshima.

The Hiroshima Experience

Hiroshima had always fascinated me. It was the city that had suffered one of the most devastating tragedies in human history—the atomic bombing during World War II. I had read about the horrors of that day and the aftermath, and I was curious to see how the city had rebuilt itself. What I found was beyond anything I had expected.

I arrived in Hiroshima expecting to see a city still bearing the scars of its tragic past, perhaps weighed down by a lingering sadness or bitterness. I also expected to encounter some resentment toward the United States for the nuclear bombings. Instead, what I found was a vibrant, thriving city full of life, energy, and optimism. Hiroshima had not only rebuilt itself physically, but it had transformed into a symbol of peace and resilience.

As I walked through the modern streets of Hiroshima, surrounded by thriving businesses, busy people, and American tourists casually taking in the sights, I was struck by the city's remarkable transformation. There were American brands everywhere, and I saw no signs of lingering animosity toward the country responsible for its darkest hour.

My curiosity led me to talk to the locals. I wanted to understand how they felt about the bombings and about the United States. Their responses were nothing short of extraordinary. Instead of anger or bitterness, they spoke with a sense of forgiveness and reconciliation. They had moved on, focusing not on the past, but on rebuilding and creating a better future.

One conversation, in particular, stood out to me. I spoke with an elderly man who had lived through the bombing. I expected him to express some level of resentment or sorrow, but instead, he told me something profound. He said that holding on to anger would only hold them back. "We chose to forgive," he said, "because it was the only way to move forward." He spoke about how the people of Hiroshima had focused on teaching the younger generation to embrace self-development, peace, and resilience, rather than dwelling on the pain of the past.

This attitude was echoed by everyone I spoke to, whether they were young or old. It was clear that Hiroshima had not just physically rebuilt itself—it had healed emotionally and spiritually. The resilience, the ability to forgive, and the unwavering focus on the future left a deep and lasting impression on me. It changed how I viewed challenges and hardships in life.

Learning Resilience from Japan

Japan's influence on me deepened after this visit. I realized that the strength of the Japanese people didn't just come from their technological advancements or efficient systems; it came from their mindset. The Japanese have a remarkable ability to face challenges head-on, to learn from their experiences, and to come out stronger on the other side. They don't dwell on the past or wallow in negative emotions. Instead, they channel their energy into Kaizen, constantly striving for improvement, both individually and as a society.

This lesson from Hiroshima had a profound effect on me. It showed me that no matter what challenges we face—whether they are personal, professional, or even national—resilience and a positive mindset are key to moving forward. The Japanese people had every reason to remain bitter about their past, but instead, they chose to focus on growth and peace. Their ability to forgive and rebuild inspired me to adopt a similar approach in my own life.

Punch line "From Hiroshima's heart to Japan's art, resilience and growth set us apart."

A Personal Philosophy

My connection with Japan had begun in the workplace, with Kaizen, 5S, and lean manufacturing, but it had grown into something much deeper. It had become a personal philosophy—a way of looking at life through the lens of continuous improvement, resilience, and the pursuit of a better future.

Japan had become my second love after my own country, India. The values and principles I learned there have stayed with me ever since, shaping how I approach both my work and my personal life. Whether it's solving a problem at work, navigating a difficult situation in my personal life, or simply improving my daily habits, the Japanese mindset of perseverance, efficiency, and positivity is something I carry with me every day.

Final Thoughts

Japan's influence on me has been profound and far-reaching. It has taught me that no matter how difficult the challenges we face, it's possible to rebuild, to grow, and to achieve greatness by focusing on development and letting go of the past. The lessons I learned from Japan—particularly from my visit to Hiroshima—have become guiding principles in my life. They've taught me the importance of resilience, the power of forgiveness, and the value of looking ahead with hope, no matter how painful the past might have been.

This journey, which began with a chance campus placement, evolved into a lifelong connection with a country whose values have shaped me in ways I never imagined. I am forever grateful for the lessons Japan has taught me, and I hope to continue applying those lessons in every aspect of my life, always striving for improvement, and embracing the resilience to overcome any challenge.

Value 34 - The Price of Fast Growth

As I reflect on my professional journey, one of the most striking aspects is how quickly I advanced in my career. At just 19, I began my career as a Junior Engineer, filled with excitement and ambition. By the age of 32, I found myself sitting in the office of a General Manager of Operations, leading teams, making decisions, and steering entire projects. Looking back, the pace at which my career unfolded fills me with pride, but it was also a journey lined with significant challenges—ones that evaluated not just my professional abilities but my resilience and mental strength.

When I started, I set a clear target for myself: to become a manager within 10 years. I remember my own manager at the time, a man who had taken 20 years to reach his position, advising me to set a high bar. "Aim to get there in 10 years," he told me, planting the seed of ambition in my mind. It was an ambitious goal, no doubt, but I was determined to achieve it. However, life had something different in store. Things moved even faster than I had anticipated. In just 8 years, I achieved that target. And before I knew it, I was a General Manager at 32—one of the youngest in my industry.

On the surface, my rapid ascent seemed like a dream come true. And in many ways, it was. But what's often overlooked are the pressures and side effects of rising through the ranks so quickly. Behind the scenes, it sparked jealousy among colleagues, stirred internal politics, and weighed heavily on my mental health—challenges that no one warned me about, but that I had to face head-on.

The Weight of Rapid Success

Imagine being in your early 30s, walking into boardrooms filled with people much older and far more experienced than you. I was leading teams where some members had decades of experience on me. Naturally, this scenario led to doubt and scepticism from others. I could feel the silent question hanging in the air: How could someone so young lead us? That doubt often turned into something more difficult to deal with—jealousy. And jealousy has a way of creeping into the workplace, making subtle but damaging appearances.

One particular moment stands out vividly in my memory. A senior colleague, someone who had been with the company for nearly 25 years, openly questioned my decisions in front of the entire team. His tone was dismissive, and his words dripped with sarcasm. It wasn't just a disagreement; it was a test of my authority and leadership. In that moment, I had two choices: to react defensively, giving him exactly what he was expecting, or to respond with calmness and confidence—the confidence that had earned me this role in the first place.

I chose the latter. I calmly explained my decision, backing it up with data and a logical approach, and then I opened the floor for further discussion. The room went quiet. There were no further questions. I had passed the test, but it wasn't a victory I celebrated. It left a mark on me. I realized that leading from a position of strength meant constantly proving myself, over and over again—not just to others, but to myself as well.

The Internal Battle

What people often don't see in someone who has climbed the ladder quickly are the invisible battles that rage beneath the surface. For every outward display of confidence, there is an internal struggle—one that includes anxiety, self-doubt, and the fear of making mistakes. Each day felt like a balancing act, trying to live up to the expectations that came with my title, while also dealing with the insecurities that came from being so young in a high-stakes role.

The pressure to perform was immense. I found myself waking up in the middle of the night, replaying decisions I had made during the day, wondering if I had missed something or if I could have managed a situation better. The constant need to justify my position wasn't just coming from my team—it was coming from within me.

At times, the mental strain was overwhelming. I kept my composure outwardly, but inside, I was exhausted. The fear of making a wrong decision, of failing in front of people who were older, more experienced, and perhaps waiting for me to stumble, weighed on me heavily.

But, as I look back now, I realize those were the moments that shaped me. The jealousy, the internal politics, the mental strain—while painful at the time—were the very challenges that forced me to grow. They made me develop a thick skin, to focus intensely on my work, and to prove myself not just through words, but through results. I learned early on that in the corporate world, your best defines is your performance. When the results speak for themselves, the noise around you begin to quiet down.

Flexibility: The Key to Thriving

Another lesson that came with this rapid rise was the importance of flexibility and adaptability. Nothing about my career had gone according to a set plan. I didn't follow a rigid path; instead, I flowed from one opportunity to the next, making decisions on the fly, adjusting to new environments, and learning new skills as I went. This ability to adapt quickly became one of my greatest strengths.

In any corporate structure, dynamics shift constantly. People come and go, markets change, and new challenges arise. My ability to stay flexible, to embrace these changes rather than resist them, became critical to my success. Whether it was learning to manage people twice my age or navigating the complexities of international business, I realized that the only way to survive—and thrive—was to be open to constant learning and to never become rigid in my thinking. This flexibility allowed me to work across industries and cultures, from Indian companies to multinational corporations from the US, France, Germany, Italy, and Singapore. Each new role and each new environment taught me something different, adding layers to my experience and sharpening my leadership skills.

Learning from the Heat

Looking back, I see those hard times—the jealousy, the internal tests, the pressure—as the heat that forged me into who I am today. It wasn't easy. In fact, it was one of the most mentally taxing periods of my life. But it was necessary. Each challenge, each moment of doubt, became a stepping stone to greater strength. I often think of that period as a process of being heated to the boiling point. The pressure kept building, and rather than breaking under it, I learned to adapt and thrive. I didn't evaporate. I became stronger, more resilient, and more focused on my goals. Today, with over two decades of experience under my belt, I can speak about these experiences with pride and confidence. I no longer feel the need to justify my place at the table—I have earned it. But the lessons from those early years have stayed with me. They taught me that no matter how fast you rise, the real growth happens in the hard times, when you're facing pressure from all sides, and yet you choose to keep moving forward.

Moving Forward

As I stand today, with 22 years of experience across some of the most respected organizations in India and abroad, I can confidently say that every challenge, every hardship, and every test was a necessary part of my journey. Each one made me stronger, more resilient, and more capable of leading with both strength and humility.

This journey, with all its highs and lows, isn't over. I continue to face challenges, but I approach them with a confidence that comes from experience. I know now that it's not the speed of your rise that matters, but how you handle yourself along the way. The pressures of leadership never truly go away, but what changes is how you face them.

So, as I continue on this path, I do so with the knowledge that whatever challenges lie ahead, they will only serve to make me stronger. And for that, I am ready.

Punch line "Rise through the fire, fuelled by desire—every challenge makes you higher!"

Value 35 – The Flow of Solutions: How Dirty Water Taught Me the Power of Problem Solving

In our early 30s, many of us begin to feel like we've finally got a handle on life. We've gained some experience, faced challenges at work, and maybe even started giving advice to others about how to solve problems. I was no different. I had always prided myself on being a systematic problem solver at work. Little did I know, my problem-solving skills were about to be evaluated in a way I hadn't expected—right at home.

It all started one Sunday morning. As I relaxed at home, enjoying the weekend, my family noticed something odd: dirty water with mud was coming out of our tap. This wasn't just slightly discoloured water; it was muddy and clearly not fit for use. Naturally, the first reaction in the household was to think the tap itself was the problem. My family was ready to replace it, assuming that would fix everything.

But I decided to step in. "Let me manage this," I told them. After all, I was always going on about how I was a problem-solving expert at work. Now was my chance to prove it at home.

Like I would at work, I grabbed a pen and paper and sat down to outline the problem. The first step was defining the issue clearly: "Dirty water is coming from the tap." Then, I began mapping out the flow of water in our house. I discovered that our water supply came from two sources: a borewell and the local water board. The local water was only supplied three days a week, and the borewell water filled in the gaps on the other days. Both sources fed into an underground sump, which stored the water before it was pumped up to an overhead tank on the terrace. From there, the water flowed through pipes to the taps throughout the house.

As I wrote everything down, something interesting occurred to me: this dirty water problem wasn't a one-time thing. It seemed to reoccur every few months. The more I thought about it, the more I realized that even though this seemed like a simple problem, it actually required careful thought and a thorough solution.

With the problem clearly defined, I moved on to the next step: analysis. I decided to use a technique we often use at work called the "5 Whys" analysis, where you keep asking "why" until you get to the root cause of the problem.

1. Why was dirty water coming from the tap?

   Because the pipes were dirty.

2. Why were the pipes dirty?

   Because dirty water had flowed through them from the overhead tank.

3. Why was the overhead tank dirty?

   Because dirty water had flowed into it from the underground sump.

4. Why was the underground sump dirty?

   Because the incoming water from the borewell carried mud, and even the local water had some dirt in it.

As I worked through the analysis, it became clear that the root cause of the problem wasn't the tap or even the pipes themselves, but rather the entire water flow system. The borewell water, which was raw and untreated, was bringing mud into the underground sump. From there, the dirty water was being pumped into the overhead tank and then into the pipes, spreading the problem throughout the house.

The solution was now obvious: we needed to address the root cause. I decided to install a strainer at the inlet to the sump to filter out the mud before it could enter the system. Additionally, we needed to do a thorough cleaning of both the underground sump and the overhead tank. I knew it would take some time, but I was confident that this approach would solve the problem for good, rather than just providing a temporary fix.

Even at some point of time being lazy, if we try to clean only the overhead tank and run the flow, again dirt will get carried from underground sump making overhead tank and pipelines dirty. So it needs serious action with maturity and patience. For our belief if we try to do which does not solve the problem at the room, do not add any value.

After a few hours of cleaning and flushing out the entire water system, we finally saw the results: clear, clean water was flowing from the taps again. The problem was solved, and more importantly, it wouldn't be coming back anytime soon.

Reflecting on this experience, I realized that this approach to problem-solving wasn't just applicable to dirty water—it was a lesson that could be applied to many aspects of life. Often, when we face problems, it's tempting to go for the quick fix, to replace the metaphorical "tap" without addressing the real issue. But just like in this situation, the real solution often requires us to dig deeper, to clean out the underlying causes, and to prevent the problem from recurring.

In life, our minds can become like those pipes—filled with negative thoughts, doubts, and worries. It's easy to blame external factors for our unhappiness or stress, just like it was easy to blame the tap for the dirty water. But if we take the time to clean out our minds through practices like yoga, meditation, or simply reflecting on our thoughts, we can prevent those negative influences from contaminating our lives. And just like with the water system, it's important not to take shortcuts. If we only clean the surface, the dirt will eventually seep back in. True problem-solving, whether in a water system or in our own minds, requires addressing the root cause with patience and maturity.

This experience at home reminded me that whether a problem is big or small, the approach to solving it remains the same: define the problem, analyse the causes, and take action that addresses the root issue. And in the process, we might just learn something valuable that applies to every aspect of our lives.

Punch Line: "From Dirty Streams to Dreams Anew, Every Problem Has a Solution in View!"

Value 36 - Embracing the Journey as a Jack of All Trades

Throughout my life, I've always found it difficult to stick to just one thing. While many people pursue mastery in a single field, I've never felt the urge to become an expert in just one area. Instead, I've embraced the idea of being a "Jack of all trades," someone who knows a little about a lot and enjoys the variety that comes with it. For me, life is not about mastering a single subject, but about exploring different fields, gaining diverse experiences, and constantly learning something new.

Some might argue that being a Jack of all trades can be a disadvantage—that without expertise, you'll never stand out. But for me, it's not about standing out in one area; it's about understanding the world from multiple perspectives. It's about being adaptable, curious, and open to whatever opportunities come my way. This mindset has shaped my professional and personal journey in ways I never expected, and it has given me a unique sense of fulfilment.

The MBA vs. MTech Mindset

To explain my outlook, I often think about the difference between two types of education: an MBA and an MTech. An MBA teaches you how to manage various aspects of a business—finance, marketing, human resources, operations, and more. It's a broad education that equips you with the tools to oversee multiple departments, each with its own unique challenges. You learn to think like a manager, balancing different needs and finding ways to bring it all together.

On the other hand, an MTech is about deep, specialized knowledge in a particular field. It's for those who want to become experts—whether in engineering, technology, or any other specific area. MTech graduates might spend years mastering one topic, becoming the point of reference for that niche.

I've always been drawn to the MBA approach. The idea of learning a little about many things, of being able to navigate different areas and pull it all together, is what excites me. I love the flexibility that comes with being a generalist—the ability to adapt to various roles and environments, to apply broad skills wherever needed. It's like being a generalist doctor who can treat all sorts of ailments—fevers, earaches, joint pains—rather than a specialist who only focuses on the eyes or teeth. The specialist is deeply knowledgeable in their field, but the generalist can address a wider range of problems, which makes them versatile and widely needed.

School Days: The Balanced Approach

This mindset of balancing interests started early in my life, even back in school. I was never the student who excelled in just one subject. I wasn't the kind of person to score 99 in one area while risking failure in another. Instead, I believed in maintaining a balance—getting a solid 50 or 60 in every subject, ensuring that I passed everything and could move forward. It might not have made me a top student, but it ensured that I progressed steadily without leaving any subject behind.

I remember watching some of my classmates focus intensely on their strongest subjects, aiming for near-perfect scores. And while they were excellent in those areas, if they neglected a weaker subject and failed, they couldn't advance to the next class. In contrast, my balanced approach helped me succeed across the board. It might not have been flashy, but it worked for me. This philosophy of spreading my efforts instead of concentrating on just one thing has stayed with me throughout my career.

A Career of Many Hats

As I look back now, I can see how this approach shaped my career in ways I hadn't initially planned. I ended up working in a variety of industries—none of them directly related to the last. Each opportunity was different, involving new manufacturing processes, management styles, and even entirely different cultures. It wasn't by design, but it aligned perfectly with my belief in being a Jack of all trades.

Every new job was a fresh adventure, filled with new experiences and challenges. I enjoyed the process of learning the basics of a new field, adapting to the environment, and then improving over time. The diversity kept me engaged and constantly learning. I thrived on the variety, knowing that I didn't need to be an expert in one field to be successful. Instead, my ability to understand a little about a lot made me versatile and adaptable—a valuable asset in any industry.

The Specialist vs. Generalist Debate

Of course, I understand that this path isn't for everyone. Many people find satisfaction and security in sticking with the same company or industry for years, even decades. These are the specialists—people who dedicate themselves to mastering their field, building their entire careers around one subject or role. There's a lot to be said for their dedication and expertise.

However, for me, the idea of staying in one company for 30 or 40 years feels a bit odd. I often wonder how someone can prove their capabilities and innovation when they've been in the same environment for so long. I admire their stability, but I also question how they would handle the outside world if they had to leave their comfort zone. I've seen people who, after leaving a long-time job, struggle to adjust to a new culture or company. Some even return to their old jobs within a year or two because they find it difficult to adapt.

In contrast, my experience as a generalist has taught me how to be flexible and adaptable. I've learned to pick up the basics quickly, understand the essentials, and then improve as I go. Whether it's adjusting to a new industry, adopting a different management style, or learning to thrive in an unfamiliar culture, I've always managed to find my footing. This adaptability has been one of my greatest strengths, allowing me to explore diverse opportunities and grow in ways I never could have if I had focused on just one area.

The Value of Adaptability

Being a Jack of all trades has given me a sense of confidence in facing the unknown. I've learned that I don't need to be an expert to succeed. What matters is the ability to learn, adapt, and grow with each new challenge. This mindset has helped me navigate through various industries, from manufacturing to finance to management. Each experience has added to my skill set, making me more versatile and better equipped to handle whatever comes next.

I've seen the value of adaptability firsthand. In a fast-changing world, being able to pivot quickly is essential. Industries evolve, technologies change, and new challenges arise all the time. Specialists might struggle to adapt when their niche becomes outdated, but generalists can navigate these shifts more easily. My career has been a testament to this—each time a door closed, another one opened, and I was ready to step through it, knowing that I could manage whatever was on the other side.

Finding Fulfilment

In the end, the choice between being a specialist or a generalist comes down to personal preference and what brings you fulfilment. For me, the joy lies in learning a little about a lot. I love the challenge of taking on something new, figuring out the basics, and then building on that foundation. It keeps me engaged, curious, and excited about what's next. There's a sense of freedom that comes with not being tied to one specific role or industry. I feel open to possibilities, always ready to embrace the next challenge. While some people find satisfaction in mastering a single subject or becoming the go-to expert in their field, I find joy in the variety. It's not the easiest path—there's always a learning curve with each new venture—but it's the one that keeps me energized and constantly growing.

The Journey Ahead

As I reflect on my journey as a Jack of all trades, I realize that this approach has given me a sense of fulfilment that I might not have found if I had chosen a more specialized path. It's allowed me to explore different industries, learn from diverse experiences, and develop a broad range of skills that have served me well in both my personal and professional life.

Looking ahead, I know that there will always be more to learn, more to explore, and more challenges to tackle. And that's what excites me the most. I don't know where the next opportunity will take me, but I'm ready for it—because as a Jack of all trades, I've learned that the journey is never predictable, but it's always rewarding. ***Punch Line: "Master of None, Yet Second to None!"***

Value 37 - My secret to Excel revealed in reputed interview!!

It was a bright, sunny morning when I was invited for an interview by a well-respected national-level business and operational excellence forum. It was a proud moment, but also a chance to reflect on my journey. The interview flowed smoothly, touching upon various topics around my career, my network, and my thoughts on business strategy.

But then, a senior professional in the room asked a question that gave me pause. He leaned forward, a thoughtful expression on his face, and said, "I have gone through your LinkedIn profile. I can see that you have a vast professional network. Fifty percent of your followers and connections are Founders, CEOs, Directors, and global leaders. Your content has received over 43 million impressions, and you've had a huge number of profile views. Above all, you've been recognized as a LinkedIn Top Voice for a long time. Can I consider this as your individual achievement? How much of your success is due to your own efforts?"

I smiled, took a brief pause to collect my thoughts, and then replied, "No, it's not just about me alone."

The room was silent for a moment as everyone waited for me to continue. I went on to explain that success is never a result of individual effort alone. "I believe success is a combination of several factors: God's plan, individual effort, and collaboration with key people. No one, no matter how talented or hardworking, can succeed entirely on their own. We all need the support, wisdom, and help of others to truly thrive. More than the people I know well, I believe many of the people I barely know, or don't know at all, have helped me in ways I may never fully understand."

I saw a few heads nod in agreement, and the interview panel leaned in, clearly intrigued by my perspective. I continued, "In my younger years, I believed I had to do everything on my own. Like many others, I subscribed to the idea that sheer willpower, confidence, and personal effort were all it took to succeed. I'd listen to motivational speeches that said, 'You can win! You are the source of your own power!' And while there's truth in that message, it's incomplete."

It took me years of maturing, failing, and learning to realize the importance of collaboration. The more I grew in my career, the clearer it became that nobody walks this journey alone. We need others—both professionally and personally—to reach our goals. That was one of the major reasons I decided to take LinkedIn seriously. It wasn't about building a network for the sake of numbers or vanity. It was about meaningful connections, collaborations, and learning from those around me. And now, here I am, years later, being recognized for something that wasn't just my doing—it was the result of collective effort.

To illustrate this point further, I shared a story that many of us learned in school. "Do you remember the story of the tortoise and the hare?" I asked, and the panel members nodded. "We all know how it ends—the tortoise wins because he's slow and steady, while the overconfident rabbit loses due to his complacency. It's a story that teaches us patience and perseverance. But let me tell you about an updated version of that story that I came across in my 30s, and it completely changed my perspective."

Now I had their full attention.

"In this version, after losing the race, the rabbit felt humiliated and decided to challenge the tortoise to another race. This time, the rabbit was fully prepared, and he ran as fast as he could without stopping. Naturally, he won by a huge margin. The tortoise, accepting his defeat, came up with a new challenge. This time, the race included a river crossing, which the rabbit couldn't manage. The tortoise won that round.

So, at this point, both the tortoise and the rabbit had won two races each. But neither was fully satisfied. They realized that in their rivalry, they were still competing as individuals, focusing on their strengths while exposing their weaknesses. So, they decided to collaborate for the final race, which included both land and water. On land, the rabbit carried the tortoise, and in the water, the tortoise carried the rabbit. Together, they completed the race faster than either could have done alone."

I paused to let the message sink in, then said, "That story hit me like a bolt of lightning. It was a profound reminder that while individual effort is important, collaboration can take you to new heights. And that's the lesson I carry with me in my professional life: We cannot succeed alone. We need the support, the ideas, and the encouragement of others to truly thrive. That's why I've never subscribed to the belief that my achievements are mine alone."

I could see many of the listeners nodding in agreement as I spoke.

"In fact," I continued, "there were many times in my life when I was at a crossroads, unsure of how to move forward. And in those moments, people I barely knew—sometimes complete strangers—helped me. It's almost miraculous, how often help comes from the most unexpected places. There are people you may never meet who have contributed to your journey in ways you may never fully understand. That's why I believe in paying it forward. I've referred over 300 people for jobs, not because I expect anything in return, but because I know how important it is to help others on their journey."

As I reflected further, I shared another key lesson I've learned over the years: the importance of unlearning. "As we grow, we need to continuously learn from others, but we also need to unlearn outdated beliefs. When I was younger, I thought success meant doing everything on my own, being self-reliant. But I had to unlearn that mindset to embrace the power of collaboration."

"I've learned to stay humble," I said, "because no matter how much we achieve, there's always more to learn from others. The moment we think we've made it on our own is the moment we stop growing. And growth, both personal and professional, is a lifelong process."

I could sense that my words resonated with the panel, especially the senior professional who had asked the initial question. He smiled as I concluded, "So, no—this isn't just my achievement. It's the result of God's plan, the efforts of countless people I've had the privilege of working with, and the power of collaboration. I'm merely a part of a much bigger picture, and for that, I'm grateful."

The atmosphere in the room had shifted. What began as a question about individual achievement had turned into a discussion on the value of teamwork, humility, and the unseen forces that contribute to our success.

As the interview came to a close, I left the room feeling lighter, having shared not just my accomplishments but also the invaluable lessons I've learned along the way. The power of collaboration, the importance of unlearning, and the gratitude for all the unseen hands that have lifted me—these are the true ingredients of success.

And as I walked out into the sunshine, I knew that the journey was far from over. There would be more challenges, more lessons, and more people to learn from. But with the right mindset, and the willingness to collaborate, there was no limit to what could be achieved.

Key Learnings:

Collaboration Over Individualism: True success comes from working with others, not just from personal effort. The rabbit and tortoise story teaches us the power of teamwork.

The Value of Unlearning: Sometimes, success means letting go of old mindsets and embracing new ways of thinking.

Helping Others: Paying it forward is key to a fulfilling professional life. The people who help you may not always be the ones you expect.

Humility: Success is never solely individual. It's important to remain humble and recognize the contributions of others.

Punch Line: "Alone, we can go fast, but together we'll last!"

Value 38 - My Dream Education System

I've been thinking a lot about the future of education, and I believe it's something that's staring us right in the face. It's a reality we need to acknowledge and embrace. Picture this: a world where the same lecture isn't repeated a thousand times across different colleges, but instead, it's delivered once by the best educator and made available to everyone, everywhere. That's the power of technology, and it's already within our reach. We're living in a time where knowledge isn't confined to a classroom or limited by geography. It's available at our fingertips, accessible anytime, anywhere. So, why are we still clinging to an outdated system that's been around for centuries?

Let's start by taking a step back and examining the current state of tertiary education in India. Universities and colleges are filled with students who attend lectures day in and day out. Often, they're receiving the same information that could easily be found online. Just think about the hours spent preparing for and delivering these lectures, only for the content to be repeated endlessly, semester after semester, across different institutions. This repetition is an inefficient use of time and resources, both for the educators who painstakingly prepare their lectures and for the students who spend hours in lecture halls.

Now, consider the world we live in today. We have platforms like YouTube, Coursera, and countless others that offer access to high-quality educational content from the best educators around the globe. So, the question arises: why do we still need to physically attend a lecture? The truth is, we don't—not in the traditional way we've been doing for so long. What we really need is a shift in focus. Instead of colleges being places where students gather to listen to the same lecture over and over, they should become hubs of research, innovation, and critical thinking. We should reserve the classroom for what truly matters—interaction, discussion, and the development of new ideas.

Here's how I envision the future of tertiary education in India. We need to move away from the traditional model of repetitive lecturing. Instead, let's create a system where the best lectures are recorded and made available online for everyone. Imagine the impact of having the most knowledgeable and engaging educators delivering their lectures just once but reaching millions of students across the country. These lectures would be delivered by experts in their fields, ensuring that all students, regardless of where they live or study, have access to the highest quality education. Once the lecture is recorded and available online, students can watch it as many times as they need, at their own pace, and on their own schedule. This not only democratizes access to education but also caters to the different learning styles and speeds of students.

But my vision doesn't stop at simply recording and sharing lectures. The future of education isn't just about watching videos—it's about creating an interactive learning experience that goes beyond passive consumption of information. Imagine a system where questions can be answered by artificial intelligence, providing instant feedback, and helping students understand complex concepts in real-time. This would free up educators to focus on what really matters—mentoring students, guiding research projects, and fostering an environment of creativity and innovation.

Think about it: a college where students don't attend lectures but instead spend their time conducting experiments, working on projects, and engaging in meaningful discussions with their peers and professors. They would be learning by doing, not just by listening. And when they need to learn about a specific topic, they can access the best lecture available on that subject, delivered by an expert who knows the material inside and out. This hands-on approach would not only deepen their understanding of the subject matter but also develop critical skills like problem-solving, collaboration, and innovation.

The benefits of this new approach to education are numerous. For one, it would make tertiary education more affordable. By reducing the need for physical classrooms and the repetition of lectures, the costs associated with education could be significantly lowered. Colleges would no longer need to charge exorbitant fees for access to information that is freely available online. Instead, they could focus on providing value through research opportunities, hands-on experience, and the development of critical thinking skills.

In this new system, colleges would transform into centres for certification and testing. They would validate the knowledge and skills that students have gained through their online lectures and self-directed learning. This would ensure that students aren't just passively consuming information but actively applying it in real-world scenarios. The emphasis would shift from rote memorization to the ability to think critically, solve problems, and innovate.

Let me give you an example. Imagine a student who wants to learn about artificial intelligence. Instead of attending a series of lectures spread out over several months, they could access a comprehensive lecture on AI delivered by a world-renowned expert. After watching the lecture and engaging with AI-powered quizzes and simulations to test their understanding, the student could then apply their knowledge in a project—perhaps developing a simple AI model or exploring the ethical implications of AI in society. When they're ready, they could take an exam or submit their project for certification. The focus here is on mastery of the subject, not just completing a course.

Another significant advantage of this model is its potential to address the issue of accessibility in education. In India, many students are unable to attend top universities due to financial constraints, geographical limitations, or a lack of infrastructure. By making high-quality educational content available online, we can ensure that every student, regardless of their background, has the opportunity to learn from the best. This would level the playing field and give every student a fair chance to succeed.

Furthermore, this new model of education encourages lifelong learning. In today's fast-paced world, the skills and knowledge we acquire during our formal education are often not enough to sustain us throughout our careers. As technology and industries evolve, so too must our knowledge and skills. In a system where learning is flexible, accessible, and self-directed, students are encouraged to continue learning throughout their lives. Whether it's through online courses, certifications, or professional development programs, the future of education will require individuals to continuously update their skills and knowledge.

Let's not forget the role of educators in this new system. In the traditional model, educators spend a significant amount of time preparing and delivering lectures. But in the future, their role will evolve into something much more impactful. Instead of being lecturers, they will become mentors and guides, helping students navigate their learning journeys. They will be there to provide personalized feedback, offer insights based on their own experiences, and inspire students to explore new ideas. This shift in focus will not only make education more effective but also more fulfilling for both educators and students.

Now, I'm not suggesting that traditional classrooms should disappear altogether. Primary and secondary education, in particular, still needs that traditional setting to ensure that students get a strong foundation in basic skills and knowledge. Younger students benefit from the structure and social interaction that a classroom provides. However, as students' progress to higher levels of education, the need for traditional classrooms diminishes. The old classroom model would gradually be phased out in favour of a more flexible, efficient, and affordable system that caters to the needs of the modern world.

This is the dream I have for the future of education in India—a system where learning is accessible, affordable, and focused on what truly matters. A system where technology is leveraged to make education more efficient and effective, where colleges become centres of innovation and critical thinking, and where students are empowered to take control of their learning journey. The traditional model of education has served us well for centuries, but it's time for a change.

The future of education is already here, and we have the tools to make it a reality. By embracing the possibilities that technology offers, we can create an education system that prepares students not just for exams, but for the challenges and opportunities of life. This new model isn't just about making education more efficient; it's about making it more meaningful. By focusing on what truly matters—critical thinking, problem-solving, and real-world application—we can ensure that students are not just prepared for exams, but for life.

In conclusion, the future of education is something we can no longer ignore. It's staring us in the face, offering us the opportunity to create a system that's more accessible, affordable, and effective than ever before. It's time we take the leap and embrace this future, not just for the sake of progress, but for the sake of the students who will shape the world of tomorrow. Let's make this vision a reality and create an education system that truly prepares our students for the challenges and opportunities of the 21st century.

Punch line: "Learn, grow, and innovate—let's make the future of education great!"

Value 39 - My realisation about Power of Leverage and True Wealth

There's a lesson I learned over the years that completely shifted the way I think about money, work, and wealth. The worst way to make money is by selling your time. You might wonder why I say this, especially since most of us are taught to find a good job and work hard to earn a living. But here's the truth—when you sell your time, no matter how much you charge, your income will always be tied to the hours you work. And that is what we call linear income.

I'll give you an example. Let's say you're a doctor, one of the highest-paid professionals in the world. You might be charging ₹1000 for just 5 minutes of consultation. That sounds great, right? But here's the catch—your income is still directly connected to the time you spend seeing patients. You can only see a certain number of patients in a day, and there's a hard limit to how much you can earn because time is a limited resource. No matter how much you charge, no matter how many hours you work, your income will always depend on your time.

Now, don't get me wrong. You can get rich by working hard and charging high rates for your time. Plenty of people do. But here's the key difference: getting rich is not the same as becoming wealthy.

Let me explain. When I say "wealthy," I'm not just talking about having a lot of money. True wealth means having the freedom to choose how you spend your time. It's the ability to do what you want, when you want, without being tied to a job, a client, or a clock. It's not just about making money; it's about having control over your life.

So how do you achieve that? You need to start thinking about non-linear income—the kind of income that keeps coming in, even when you're not actively working. This is what allows you to earn money while you sleep, while you're on vacation, or even while you're spending time with your family. This is the kind of income that leads to true wealth because it's not tied to your hours or your effort. It's scalable, meaning it can grow without any extra input from you.

Here's the amazing thing: we are the luckiest generation in the history of humanity. Why? Because we live in an age of unlimited leverage—something our ancestors never had. Leverage is what allows you to multiply your output without multiplying your effort. It's the secret to creating non-linear income and achieving the kind of financial freedom that leads to real wealth.

There are three types of leverage you can use to create this kind of income and understanding them is crucial.

1. Leverage Through Labor

The first type of leverage is labour, which is the oldest form of leverage. This is when you hire people to work for you, and their efforts multiply your productivity. Think of a business owner who employs a team of workers. Instead of doing all the work themselves, they delegate tasks to their employees, and together they achieve far more than any one person could alone.

Labor leverage has been around for centuries, and it's still powerful. But it has its limitations. Managing people can be time-consuming, and there's only so much you can scale with human effort. You need to pay salaries, provide training, and deal with the complexities of managing a team.

That's why, while labour is a good form of leverage, it's not the most efficient one in today's world.

2. Leverage Through Capital

The second type of leverage is capital. This is when you use money to make more money. For example, when you invest in stocks, real estate, or businesses, you are using capital leverage. You're putting your money to work, and ideally, it grows without you having to do much once the investment is made.

Capital leverage can be incredibly powerful. It's how the wealthy get wealthier because they let their money compound over time. If you invest wisely, your money works for you, and you can earn returns without having to work harder.

But there's a barrier to capital leverage—you need money to begin with. You can't leverage capital if you don't have any. This is why many people feel stuck, working jobs they don't love, just to save up enough money to invest.

3. Leverage Through Digital Products

Now, here's the real game-changer: the third type of leverage is digital leverage, and it is by far the most powerful form of leverage in the world today. Digital leverage is what allows you to create something once and have it work for you forever, without any additional effort.

This could be a piece of software, a digital product, or even content like an online course or a YouTube video. You create it once, and it can reach millions of people. The beauty of digital products is that they are infinitely scalable. There is no limit to how many people can download a piece of software, watch a video, or read an article online. And the best part? Once it's created, it can continue to generate income for you without any additional work.

This is the kind of non-linear income that can truly make you wealthy. You're no longer trading your time for money; you're trading your creativity and ideas for income that can scale infinitely.

In today's world, you don't need a factory, a huge workforce, or massive amounts of capital to create wealth. All you need is an internet connection, some creativity, and the willingness to leverage digital tools. We live in a time where anyone, regardless of their background, can create something of value that reaches the entire world.

The Ultimate Return on Investment: Freedom

At the end of the day, the goal of all this is freedom. Freedom is the ultimate form of wealth. When you have freedom, you can choose how you spend your time. You're not tied to a job or a schedule. You can pursue your passions, spend time with loved ones, travel, or simply enjoy life on your own terms.

Money is just a tool to get there. It's not the end goal. The real goal is to create a life where you have control over your time. That's why it's so important to think beyond just making money. You need to focus on creating income that works for you, instead of working for your income.

So, as you think about your own life and career, ask yourself this: Are you working for money, or is your money working for you? If you're still trading your time for money, it's time to start thinking about how you can create leverage in your life. Whether it's through labour, capital, or digital products, the key is to create a system that allows you to earn non-linear income, so you can finally achieve the kind of financial freedom that leads to true wealth.

And remember, true wealth isn't about how much money you have in the bank. It's about having the freedom to choose how you spend your time. It's about waking up in the morning and deciding what you want to do with your day, not what you have to do. That, to me, is the real definition of success.

We are living in a unique moment in history where unlimited leverage is at our fingertips. The opportunities are endless, and the only limits are the ones we place on ourselves. So, take advantage of this moment. Find a way to create something that can scale without your constant involvement. Start building towards non-linear income and watch as your life transforms from one of hard work to one of true freedom.

Because at the end of the day, wealth is not measured in money—it's measured in freedom.

Punch Line: "Leverage the power, rise above the fray—True wealth grows stronger, shared along the way!"

Value 40 - Being Marketing Manager for Self!!

It was just another weekday morning. The city was still waking up, and the roads were crowded with people making their way to work. I was on my regular carpool to the office, a daily routine that had become almost meditative—a time to reflect, share thoughts, and sometimes, dive into deeper conversations with my carpool mates. That day, however, the atmosphere inside the car felt different. One of my friends, who usually had plenty to say, was unusually quiet. His eyes were focused on the road ahead, but I could sense his mind was elsewhere, preoccupied with something heavy.

After a long stretch of silence, he finally opened up. "I don't know, man. I just feel... invisible," he said, his voice tinged with frustration. "It's like, no matter what I do, nobody seems to notice. Not at work, not even in my personal life. I work hard, I achieve things, but it feels like nobody cares. And the worst part is, I feel like I can't even talk about it. If I start telling people what I've accomplished, it'll just sound like I'm boasting. Or worse, it might attract jealousy or the evil eye."

As he spoke, his words resonated deeply with me, stirring up memories from a time in my life when I had felt exactly the same. Between the ages of 19 and 27, I went through a similar struggle. I was full of ambition and drive, always pushing myself to achieve more, to do better. And yet, I rarely, if ever, spoke about my accomplishments. I thought that by staying humble; by not drawing attention to myself, I was doing the right thing. But in reality, I was only burying my successes, hiding them from the world as if they were something to be ashamed of.

During those years, I achieved many things that I was proud of—things that took immense effort, dedication, and resilience. I helped hundreds of people find jobs, connected with influential figures in my industry, and even became a recognized voice on LinkedIn, where industry legends followed me. My professional network grew large and strong, filled with individuals who valued my insights and contributions. But despite all of this, I kept quiet about it. Even my own family had no idea of the extent of what I had accomplished. I didn't share my successes, didn't celebrate them publicly, and certainly didn't seek recognition for them.

Looking back now, I realize how misguided I was. It wasn't humility that kept me silent; it was fear. Fear of being judged, of being seen as arrogant or self-centred. I worried that if I spoke about my achievements, people would think less of me, or that they would envy me. And so, I remained in the shadows, content to let my work speak for itself. But the truth is, the world is often too busy, too distracted, to notice even the most remarkable efforts unless they are brought to light.

It wasn't until much later that I had a revelation—one that changed the way I approached both my personal and professional life. I realized that if we've worked hard, if we've achieved something significant, then we have every right to share it with others. Not out of vanity, but out of a desire to be seen, to be acknowledged for the contributions we've made. And this isn't just about receiving praise or admiration; it's about ensuring that our efforts are recognized and remembered, that they have a lasting impact.

One of the most poignant moments that solidified this understanding for me was the death of a colleague of mine. He was a young man, full of potential, whose life was cut tragically short. At his cremation, I was struck by the sheer number of people who attended—many of whom his family and closest friends didn't even know. These people shared stories of how he had helped them, how he had made a difference in their lives in ways big and small. They spoke of his kindness, his generosity, and his unwavering support. But as I stood there listening, I couldn't help but feel a deep sadness. These were things he should have heard while he was alive. The recognition, the gratitude, the acknowledgment—all of it came too late.

What's the use of being celebrated after we're gone, when we can no longer appreciate it? Why should our worth be recognized only in retrospect, when we're no longer around to feel the joy and satisfaction that comes from knowing we made a difference? This experience, along with many others, taught me a critical lesson: No matter what position we hold in life, whether it's in our personal relationships or in our careers, we must become our own advocates. We must be the ones to tell our stories, to highlight our achievements, and to ensure that our efforts are not overlooked.

This doesn't mean we should be constantly bragging about every little thing we do. There's a fine line between self-promotion and arrogance, and it's important to navigate that line with care. The key is to develop a level of maturity that allows us to share our successes in a way that is both meaningful and appropriate. We don't need to update the world on every minor accomplishment, but we should make it a point to highlight the key milestones in our lives—the moments that truly define who we are and what we've achieved.

I've come to understand that when I talk about my accomplishments, there will always be people who feel envious or who might even try to bring me down. But I've learned not to let that deter me. I've already lost too many years to silence, and I refuse to lose any more. Even writing this book, a project that is deeply personal to me, might raise questions among those in my inner circle. They might wonder, "What's so special that he's writing a book about it?" But as I mentioned at the beginning of this journey, this book isn't for them—it's for me. It's my way of documenting my life, of ensuring that my story is told, and that my experiences and insights are preserved.

I don't want to end up like my colleague, whose contributions were only recognized after his death. I want to live my life fully, with the knowledge that my efforts are seen and valued. And I want to encourage others to do the same. If you've worked hard, if you've achieved something significant, don't be afraid to share it. The world won't always notice on its own. It's up to you to make sure your contributions are acknowledged.

In the same vein, I believe it's important for those who have received help or support from others to express their gratitude. Don't wait until it's too late to say thank you. Show your appreciation while the person is still around to hear it. We never know when someone might leave this world, and once they're gone, the opportunity to express your gratitude is lost forever.

So, as you navigate your own journey, remember this: Don't shy away from sharing your successes. Don't let fear or doubt keep you from celebrating your achievements. Be proud of what you've accomplished, and don't hesitate to let others know about it. The world is full of distractions, and if you don't tell your story, it might never be told. And that would be a loss not just for you, but for everyone who could have been inspired, uplifted, or impacted by your journey.

In the end, life is about more than just living—it's about leaving a legacy. And that legacy should be one that is celebrated, recognized, and remembered. So, speak up, share your story, and ensure that your efforts don't go unnoticed. Because you deserve to be seen, to be acknowledged, and to be valued for all that you've done.

Punch Line: "Building my brand, with a vision so grand!"

Thank Note: A Journey of Gratitude and Continuation

As I sit here, reflecting on the past forty years of my life, I am filled with a deep sense of satisfaction and contentment. Reaching this milestone has allowed me to pause and look back at the journey that has shaped me into the person I am today. Life, with all its twists and turns, has been a beautiful, complex, and rewarding experience. This book, which I have poured my heart into, is not just a collection of memories, but a celebration of those moments—good and bad—that have made my life meaningful.

I am not writing this for fame or recognition. I don't know how many people will ever pick up this memoir and read it, but that was never my goal. This book is for me, a gift to my forty-year-old self, a tangible reminder of where I've been, what I've seen, and who I've become. One day, maybe years from now, I will sit down and read these words again, and I will smile. I will smile at the memories, the lessons, and the journey. And in that moment, I will be reminded of why I wrote this—because every life is worth documenting, especially our own.

Over the years, I have been incredibly fortunate to be surrounded by love and support. I owe so much to my parents, who were the foundation upon which I built my life. Their sacrifices, their wisdom, and their unwavering belief in me allowed me to dream big and pursue my goals with confidence. My parents taught me the values of hard work, compassion, and resilience, and those lessons have been the guiding principles of my life. As I look back, I realize how deeply grateful I am for their presence and influence. They have been my greatest teachers, showing me the importance of love, family, and kindness.

I am equally thankful for my friends, those companions who have walked with me through the various phases of my life. Some friendships have lasted decades, while others were brief but impactful. Each one has added a unique layer to my story, enriching my life in ways I could never have imagined. From childhood companions to colleagues who became confidants, these relationships have been a source of joy, laughter, and sometimes even pain. But all of it was necessary. My friends have been my sounding boards, my shoulders to cry on, and my partners in crime. Without them, my journey would have been much lonelier and far less colourful.

Then there are the teachers and mentors, the gurus who have shown me the way when I felt lost or unsure of myself. Their guidance has been invaluable, whether it came in the form of formal education or life lessons learned through conversation and example. Some of these mentors I met in classrooms, others in the larger classroom of life, but each has played a pivotal role in shaping my understanding of the world and myself. I carry their lessons with me every day, and I am eternally grateful for their wisdom and generosity.

My community, too, has been an essential part of my journey. The sense of belonging that comes from being part of something larger than myself has given me strength in times of doubt and joy in times of celebration. It is easy to forget how much we rely on the people around us, but my community—whether local or extended—has been a constant source of support. In return, I hope I have given back even a fraction of what I have received. It is in this mutual exchange that I have found a sense of purpose and fulfilment.

As I reflect on all these relationships and experiences, one word keeps coming to mind: gratitude. I am thankful for every person, every moment, and every opportunity that has come my way.

Life is not always easy, and it hasn't been for me either. But through it all, I have come to see that the challenges were just as important as the victories. They taught me resilience, patience, and humility. And for that, I am grateful.

I cannot talk about gratitude without acknowledging the role that faith and God have played in my life. Though my relationship with God has evolved over the years, one thing has remained constant—my belief that there is a higher power guiding us through the ups and downs of life. I have seen too many coincidences and felt too much comfort in times of despair to believe otherwise. Whether in moments of quiet prayer or loud cries for help, I have always found solace in the idea that I am not alone on this journey. For that, I am thankful beyond words.

Now, as I sit here having completed this book, I feel a sense of accomplishment. I did it. I set out to document my life, to capture the essence of these forty years, and I succeeded. This was not an easy task; it required time, reflection, and sometimes the courage to face difficult memories. But I am proud of what I've written, and I am even more excited about what lies ahead.

This is not the end of my story. In fact, it feels like just the beginning of a new chapter, one that I am eager to live and document in the future. I know there are many more experiences to come, many more lessons to learn, and many more moments to cherish. Writing this book has sparked something inside me—a desire to continue sharing my story. I have so much more to say, so many more thoughts and ideas to explore. Who knows? Maybe this will be the first of many books that come from me.

And so, dear reader if you've come this far, I want to thank you. Thank you for taking the time to walk alongside me in this journey. I hope that in some way, my story has resonated with you. And if I may leave you with one final thought, it is this:

your life is worth documenting, too. You don't have to be a celebrity or a public figure for your story to matter. Each of us has a unique journey filled with lessons, love, challenges, and triumphs. Don't wait for someone else to come along and ask you to share it. Write it down, for yourself and for those who come after you.

One day, long after we are gone, our stories will be the only way future generations will know who we were and what we stood for. It's not about fame or recognition. It's about leaving a legacy, not in the traditional sense, but in the form of memories and wisdom that can inspire and guide others. So, take a moment to reflect on your own journey, and consider putting it into words. Even if only your family or a handful of people ever read it, it will be worth it.

As I close this chapter, I do so with a full heart and an open mind, ready for whatever comes next. This journey is far from over—it is merely continuing. There are more paths to walk, more stories to live, and more reflections to be had.

That's it... 40th Birthday 40 Reflections in 40,000 words…

the journey continues...

www.ingramcontent.com/pod-product-compliance
Lightning Source LLC
LaVergne TN
LVHW041203150826
845673LV00001B/267

* 9 7 9 8 8 9 6 7 3 0 3 8 5 *